no time for sex

about the authors

Claudia Arp and David Arp, MSW, a husband-wife team, are founders and directors of Marriage Alive International, a ground-breaking ministry dedicated to providing resources and training to empower churches to help build better marriages and families. Their Marriage Alive seminar is popular across the United States and in Europe.

David received a master of science in social work from the University of Tennessee, and Claudia holds a bachelor of science in education from the University of Georgia.

The Arps are popular conference speakers, columnists, and authors of numerous books and video curricula, including the 10 Great Dates series, *Answering the 8 Cries of the Spirited Child* and the Gold Medallion Award–winning *Second Half of Marriage.*

The Arps have appeared on NBC's *Today Show, CBS This Morning,* and *Focus on the Family.*

David and Claudia have been married for more than forty years and have three married sons and eight grandchildren and live in Great Falls, Virginia.

For more information please visit their Web site: www.marriagealive.com.

David and Claudia Arp

no time for sex

finding the time you need
for getting the love you want

Our purpose at Howard Publishing is to:

- *Increase faith* in the hearts of growing Christians
- *Inspire holiness* in the lives of believers
- *Instill hope* in the hearts of struggling people everywhere
  Because He's coming again!

No Time for Sex © 2004 by David and Claudia Arp
All rights reserved. Printed in the United States of America

Published by Howard Publishing Co., Inc.
3117 North 7th Street, West Monroe, LA 71291-2227
www.howardpublishing.com
In association with the literary agency of Alive Communications, Inc.
7680 Goddard Street, Suite 200, Colorado Springs, CO 80920

04 05 06 07 08 09 10 11 12 13   10 9 8 7 6 5 4 3 2 1

Edited by Michele Buckingham
Interior design by John Mark Luke Designs
Cover design by LinDee Loveland
Library of Congress Cataloging-In-Publication Data

Arp, Dave.
 No time for sex: finding the time you need for getting the love you want/ David and Claudia Arp.
   p. cm.
 Includes bibliographical references.
 ISBN: 1-58229-400-3
 1. Sex in marriage. 2. Marriage. 3. Married people—Time management. 4. Couples—Time management. I. Arp, Claudia. II. Title.
 HQ734.A6894 2004
 646.7'8—dc22
                2004054284

To the participants

in our Marriage Alive seminars

contents

Contents

acknowledgments

We are deeply indebted to the many people who contributed to this book and gratefully acknowledge the contributions of the following people:

To those who participated in our Love, Sex, and Marriage survey; thank you for sharing your questions, concerns, struggles, stories, and helpful tips for building a creative love-life in a time-starved world.

To those who have pioneered marriage education and on whose shoulders we stand; including David and Vera Mace, David Olson, Sherod Miller, John Gottman, Les and Leslie Parrott, Emily and Dennis Lowe, Joyce and Clifford Penner, Gary Smalley, Michelle Werner Davis, Mike and Harriet McManus, and our friends at PREP, including Scott Stanley, Howard Markman, Susan Blumberg, and Natalie Jenkins. We especially thank Dianne Sollee for all she has done and is doing to encourage marriage education.

To the many other researchers and authors from whom we quoted, for your sound work that gives a solid base for the cause of marriage education.

To our Howard Publishing team, who have believed and supported this project with great enthusiasm; we especially thank our publisher, John Howard; our editors, Philis Boultinghouse and Michele Buckingham, for their excellent editorial work; Denny Boultinghouse for his vision for this book; and Gary Myers for his great efforts to get the word out about this book.

To Lee Hough and Rick Christian of Alive Communications, for being our advocate and encouraging us along the way.

part
1

in no time at all...

You can understand your situation
and start finding time for love!

living in a time-starved world

"Life isn't fair!" I (Claudia) moaned, tears welling up in my eyes. Equally frustrated, Dave stared at me in silence. What did we do to deserve this stormy night? Our boys were supposed to be away on a Boy Scout campout, and Dave and I were supposed to be enjoying a romantic evening at a bed-and-breakfast. But an unexpected tornado alert canceled the Boy Scout trip—which canceled our chance to slip away too.

This evening should have been different! We had plans. Our sons should have been snug in their sleeping bags, not home with us. The night should have been ours—but it wasn't. The tornado alert changed everything. Loud thunder, lightning bolts, and waves of hard rain crashing against the windowpanes outside only served to remind us: *another missed opportunity.*

Life seems to be full of tornadoes, doesn't it? Unforeseen time-robbers add to the stress of our already overscheduled lives. "When we get over the next hump," we tell our spouses, "we'll have time for loving each other." But after each hump is another hump, and then another. When we do find just-the-two-of-us time at the end of a busy day, we usually fall into bed exhausted—and certainly not in the mood for sex. (Well, at least one of us isn't in the mood, which only creates more stress!)

Back to that stormy night. Our love life had been time-starved for a while. Dave had just completed a huge project at work that had consumed him for months. I had been parenting solo while trying to finish a writing project. Both of us were counting on having just one evening alone. "Hope deferred makes the heart sick," wrote Solomon (Proverbs 13:12), and he could have been describing us. We had hoped to grab just one night away together, but it wasn't to be. We were heartsick.

When would we get another chance? The immediate future didn't look promising. The grandparents were coming in a couple of days, and we needed to get ready for their visit. We had menus to plan, grocery lists to make, bills to be paid. Not to mention, our house was a disaster.

All we wanted was twenty-four hours to relax and love each other before company arrived and things really got hectic. But there was no time for a love life. There was no time for sex!

Time Zappers

Time. Such a significant factor in any love life, and yet most married couples seem to have so little of it! Time zappers come in all shapes and sizes. Kids, careers, conflict, poor communication, disorganization, overcommitment, minutiae—the list of culprits that zap our time and energy is endless. As a result, many couples today are DINS—"Double Income, No Sex." Some are DINSNH—"Double Income, No Sex, No Hope."

Jeremy and Page are one of those DINS couples. Cofounders of a very successful consulting business, they enjoy the challenge of working and building a business together, but they often bring their work home with them.

"Our life is ridiculous," Page told us. "All day yesterday we worked on a proposal that should have been completed last week. When we didn't get it finished at the office, we brought it home with us. At about ten o'clock we realized we hadn't eaten dinner, so we quickly consumed two Power Bars and continued to work until one o'clock in the morning. I'd like to say this kind of schedule is the exception, but too often it's the norm. Our typical day leaves no time for amorous feelings of any kind—much less sex!"

Today, most couples live life at mach speed. At least Jeremy and Page work together. Neil and Lauren don't. Neil is an attorney and on track to make partner. Lauren runs an interior-decorating business. They both want to support and encourage each other in their careers, but they miss the relaxed times they used to have together in the less hectic days (relatively speaking) when Neil was in law school and Lauren was an executive secretary. Back then, they had time for loving each other. But now—time for sex? Don't count on it!

Sometimes time-starved marriages are the result of poor communication. Jenny and Dustin care deeply for each other, but Jenny, a substitute teacher, feels that she and her husband, a full-time financial planner, don't spend enough time together. She continually tries to get Dustin to spend more time with her, but when she pursues him, he feels threatened and withdraws. Then, knowing that he has let his wife down, he pulls back even further and puts in more hours at the office. The sad thing is, Dustin would really like to spend more time with Jenny. He just never expresses how he really feels. Many time-starved couples fall into this pursuer/withdrawer pattern.

Then there's the "kids factor." Recently our friend Julie exclaimed, "You tried to tell me what it would be like after our son, Jason, was born. You told me I would be frazzled and exhausted, that Frank and I would have to fight for time alone, and that we would even ignore our dog. I just didn't believe you!

"I really thought I could have it all—marriage, motherhood, a fulfilling career—*and* a love life. But now I wonder, what happened to ours? Date nights are vague memories. We've become so child-focused that our marriage and our sex life are on the back burner, simmering and waiting to boil over."

Do you identify with any of these couples? If you're married, you probably do! Time starvation is a universal marital issue. In his book *A Strong Family*, Bill Doherty, director of the Marriage and Family Therapy Program at the University of Minnesota, reminds us that if couples feel deeply for one another, they are likely to feel time-starved. Couples who don't yearn for more time together are generally the ones who don't like each other anymore![1]

Natural Birth Control

Most of us, especially during the parenting years, live with a chronic deficit in the amount of time we spend with our spouses. This was definitely our experience.

Our marriage became time-starved when the first baby arrived. Never did we dream how much one little baby could affect our relationship and our love life! We had been married for almost four years when this six-pound-seven-ounce bundle of dynamite invaded our home. It was the equivalent of someone rolling a live hand grenade under our bed. The explosion blew away our sex life and caused mass confusion!

As new parents we were overwhelmed, exhausted, and insecure. We kept waiting for life to return to normal. It never did. When I went back for my six-week postpartum check-up, the doctor told me we could resume sex as usual. Who was he kidding? After the birth of each of our sons, it was several months before sex (for me anyway) was even comfortable, much less enjoyable. And it was a rare occasion indeed when we weren't too tired to even attempt it.

With the addition of two more kids, life began to spin out of control. We had almost given up on both sleep and sex at that point. To make matters worse, our sexual desires for each other were out of sync. I would crawl into bed after the late-night feeding of son number three only to find Dave, the night owl, ready for the loving to begin. Fat chance! Then there would be those early mornings when I, the morning lark, would wake up in an amorous mood; but because Dave had walked the floor until 4:00 a.m. with our newest bundle of joy, I couldn't shake him out of his deep slumber. We began to suspect that babies were actually a method of natural birth control! At that point, we would have gladly traded our sex life for the rare pleasure of eight hours of uninterrupted sleep. (At least one of us would have.)

Gone were those relaxed and enjoyable times-for-two we'd known BC (before children). We forgot what it was like to have uninterrupted time to talk, love, and dream together. Leisurely hours of romancing, cuddling, and making one another feel cherished were vague memories. Everyday intimacy—so familiar before our sons joined our family—was missing now. Don't get us wrong; we loved our sons and we loved being parents, but we longed for the easygoing communication and physical closeness that filled the first years of our marriage.

Many years have passed since that stormy night when the

tornado alert foiled our plans for love. Now the boys are grown and gone, and we live in the proverbial empty nest. So time for sex isn't an issue anymore, right? Wrong! We still have to fight our workaholic tendencies. We have a heavy travel schedule, leading seminars around the country. And since our office is in our home, we work at home too. Sometimes we struggle to put our work aside even to take time to eat.

We understand time starvation. It's as much of a struggle for us now as ever. But we're convinced that while living in a time-starved world is challenging, it shouldn't make couples celibate! That's why we've written this book. We want to help you understand and assess your own unique situation and find the time you need to get the love you want.

Maybe the vital love life you had in the beginning of your marriage—before kids, careers, and other time zappers—is in low-maintenance, survival mode. You have a flickering memory of what was and what might be again. Or maybe your love life wasn't so great to begin with, and the time zappers have made you lose all hope.

Whatever your situation, we have good news. Chronically busy husbands and wives *can* find time for love, romance, and sex. In the following pages, we'll tell you how. From our own experience of parenting three boys, pursuing dual careers, and working for two decades with couples in Marriage Alive seminars, along with the experiences of those who participated in our national "Love, Marriage, and Sex" survey, we've learned a few secrets about having a great love life. We want to share those secrets with you.[2]

Great Sex

You can have great sex—even in a time-starved world. You can develop, maintain, and revitalize a great love life. But you have to have the right attitude. You have to be intentional about it. Understand, when we talk about sex, we're talking about much more than sexual intercourse. We're talking about developing and nurturing a love life, not just finding ten minutes here or there for physical release. As one woman told us, "I want time for intimacy—for leisurely backrubs and cups of tea before making love. You can't do that in ten minutes after the news."

Especially for a wife, a fulfilling love life is multidimensional. A husband needs to understand that his mate's desire for tenderness, for feeling loved, cherished, and romanced, is as integral as his desire for passion, excitement, and physical fulfillment. Great sex is God's good gift to marriage, and great sex involves it all: tenderness, love, romance, passion, excitement. And it's fulfilling physically, emotionally, and spiritually.

It's also good for your marital health. In her book *The Sex-Starved Marriage*, Michele Weiner-Davis writes, "Sex is an extremely important part of marriage. When it's good, it offers couples opportunities to give and receive physical pleasure, to connect emotionally and spiritually. It builds closeness, intimacy, and a sense of partnership. It defines their relationship as different from all others. Sex is a powerful tie that binds."[3]

Finding time for building a great love life requires sacrifice. Maybe you're balancing on the two-job tightrope. Maybe you're in the middle of the hectic parenting years. Maybe other responsibilities, commitments, or personal issues are robbing you of quality time with your spouse. As you go through different seasons of life, you will need to continually make adjustments.

While having kids added to our own time deprivation, after a while we weren't quite so exhausted; and with stubborn determination, we found ways to stay connected. Eventually, our sex life rebounded. But it didn't happen overnight—not even in a few months. If you and your spouse are new parents, just how long your own journey back to a healthy sex life will take depends on many factors: the type and difficulty of birth, the temperament of your child, your own temperaments, the degree of support you get from family and others, and of course, your job situation. But you can do it. You can build a healthy, creative love life!

In the following pages we will consider how a healthy marriage and a healthy lifestyle are the prerequisites to a great sex life. Then we will identify the basic building blocks of any healthy relationship: positive communication, encouragement, shared core beliefs, and commitment to growth. We'll talk about expectations—your own and your spouse's—so you both can be more understanding of one another and more sexually responsive. Afterward, we will tackle the two biggest barriers to loving your partner: lack of time and lack of energy. And what about those lovely little products of family planning? We'll talk about how you can teach your children to respect your marriage and your need for time alone as a couple.

Learning to have fun together is an essential component of any healthy marriage. To that end, we'll give you tips for planning getaways and finding daily "minimoments" for loving. And then we'll help you come up with your own personalized strategy for loving each other for a lifetime.

We realize that if you're like most busy spouses, you will probably be interrupted in the next five minutes. Don't let that stop you from getting started. You don't have to read the whole book, or even a whole chapter, in one sitting. Feel free to nibble your way through the pages for a quick snack when you can't find time for a more leisurely feast. The important thing is to begin! Now is the time to *make* time to build a love life that will remain vital throughout all the seasons of your marriage. Now is the time to make time for sex.

chapter

2

what is a love life anyway?

We had just begun the session in our Marriage Alive seminar called "Building a Creative Love Life" when a participant asked in sheer frustration, "What love life? I don't even have a life, much less a love life! For me, life is too complex—the children, our own parents, jobs, church, the yard. I feel as if I'm stuck in the fast lane with no way to slow down. Love life? I'd just like to have two hours alone!"

We were happy to tell her (and you as well): there is hope! Even in a time-starved world, you can overcome the barriers and develop a fully satisfying, high-priority love life.

Of course, in a perfect world, couples would have all the time they want for long walks and romantic evenings of love-making. They'd have all the time they need to talk, share, and work through issues. But the reality is, most of us have a deficit of time, not a surplus. Our time is limited. That means that when it comes to our love lives, we have to use the time we have wisely and major in the majors.

What are the "majors"? Well, if you're a parent, you'd probably say that your basic goals for your children—your "majors"—are to keep them safe, fed, and healthy. Your goals for your marriage should be the same: creating a safe environment, providing regular nourishment, and maintaining overall good health.

The goal of this chapter is to help you put your finger on the pulse of your love life. How healthy is your marriage? Are you majoring in the majors? What essential "vitamins" are you missing?

Sentimental Journey

Take a trip with us for a moment. Think back to those magical moments when you and your spouse first discovered your love for one another. Do you remember the chemistry? The tingle when you held hands? That first kiss? The intense desire to be intimate with each other?

Everything comes so naturally at the beginning of a relationship! All I wanted to do was to be with Claudia. All she wanted to do was to be with me. Since I was in college at Georgia Tech in Atlanta and Claudia was at the University of Georgia in Athens, our thoughts were consumed with trying to figure out how we could get together. And our private times together were so easy. Sure, we had long conversations, but the icing on the cake was the cuddles, kisses, handholding, and hugs. We didn't need to evaluate or discuss our expectations and desires, because everything was simple. At that point there was only one essential component to our love life: being together.

Then we got married, and things changed. We no longer had to scheme to get together. That was great! But our love life was not simply about being together anymore. Like most couples, we found that we had entered marriage with different backgrounds, attitudes, and baggage to unpack and process. We understood very little about gender differences and our different biological and psychological drives. All of these factors complicated our love life.

The intense desire for romance and togetherness that we felt before marriage was replaced by a more complicated set of needs and desires: to be understood, to be recognized, to be respected as individuals. Emotional contact became just as important as physical contact.

The truth is, a healthy love life blends both the emotional, physical, and spiritual sides of love. It's like a diamond with many facets. Which facet gleams at any given moment depends upon how you are looking at the diamond and the type of light enhancing it. While the intense physical desire for sex is one facet of love, many other wonderful facets exist. When viewed together, they create a single, multifaceted jewel of great depth and beauty.

Components of a Healthy Love Life

In our marriage survey, we asked successful couples what they considered to be the best aspects of their love lives. How did they manage to have kids, jobs, other interest and activities, and a love life too? While the responses were varied, several themes emerged as essential components for a truly healthy love life: trust, mutuality, honesty, intimacy, pleasure, and sex. These are the facets of the marriage diamond, if you will—the framework for a diamond-studded love life. Let's move in closer and take a look at each of these facets individually.

Trust: Feeling Safe with Each Other

Trust is a basic component of any friendship. It's essential in a romantic relationship and foundational for the lifelong health of a marriage. You must trust that you are safe with your partner, that your partner will not harm you or betray you, and that you can share your most prized possession—yourself— with him or her. If you don't trust each other, you will spend large blocks of time trying to figure out if you have each other's best interests at heart. Mutual trust is a time saver!

Let's be realistic, though. In a relationship that's as close and as long-term as marriage, partners *will* let each other down from time to time. Maybe you've been shouldering most of the parenting and household responsibilities. Your mate keeps promising to help, but it just never seems to happen. Or maybe at a recent dinner party, your spouse inadvertently commented on the extra ten pounds you can't seem to lose. Maybe he or she made plans to do something with friends on a night you'd agreed to spend alone together. While these may not qualify as huge betrayals, they can chip away at the trust factor if they are habitual, not just occasional, occurrences.

The next time trust is broken, talk about it. Tell your partner how you feel: "Last night when you fell asleep in the middle of the video, I was disappointed. Before dinner I thought you were sending out signals that you wanted to make love—then you went to sleep." Talking about your frustrations and feelings will help your partner know that you're

Something to Ponder

Women are usually more comfortable sharing details about their lives and relationships with their close friends than men are. Most men would never even broach such personal subjects with their buddies! And they would be hurt if they knew what their wives were saying in phone calls or over cups of coffee. They might even consider the conversations a breach of trust or act of disloyalty. Ladies: Even though he's not there to hear you, keep your husband's feelings in mind when you consider whether or not to divulge personal matters to your friends.

—Dave

willing to work at finding solutions. Just the simple act of talking openly builds trust.

Brainstorm together and suggest ways you can avoid trust-busters in the future. Perhaps your spouse needs a reminder when he or she is about to break trust. Or maybe you need to set more realistic expectations. (At the Arp house, we know that if we turn on the TV or pop in a DVD at the end of a long, busy day, one of us will soon be sound asleep—even if we had other, more romantic intentions.) Constantly work to build and affirm trust between you and your spouse. Here are a few proven trust-builders to get you started:

- Say you are going to take the trash out—and actually do it.
- Notice and help out when your partner is on overload.
- Give your mate an honest compliment.
- Apologize when you are wrong.
- Accept your spouse's apology without saying, "I told you so."
- Keep your humor when the wee ones have exhausted you.

When present, trust is easily taken for granted; when absent, it's devastating. If there has been a serious breach of trust in your marriage—such as lying, cheating, or carrying on an emotional affair with a coworker—know this: Trust *can* be rebuilt, but it takes work and commitment on the part of both partners. Trust is foundational; that means you need to rebuild trust before you can work on the other aspects of your love relationship. Don't be afraid to enlist the assistance of a professional counselor or pastor. Sometimes the best gift you can give your marriage is getting some short-term professional help.

Affirming the Bond of Trust

Make a list of reasons you trust your spouse, using your spouse's name as an acrostic. For each letter give a character quality that promotes trust. For instance, here's one I wrote for Dave: I trust you because you . . .

D - Dare to always be truthful

A - Affirm your absolute loyalty to our marriage

V - Value our relationship above all others

E - Energize our relationship with fun and laughter

—Claudia

Mutuality: Freely Choosing to Love Each Other

For a marriage to be healthy, each partner must *want* to be in the relationship. Mutuality involves a decision by you and your spouse to choose each other above all others and to make your relationship a priority. It involves a mutual willingness to grow together and to adapt to each other's changing needs over the years. When you know that you and your partner are mutually committed to one another, you don't have to use up precious time continually evaluating the relationship, asking: "Does he really love me?" or "Is she going to hang in there?"

19

We all know what it feels like to be with someone who doesn't want to be with us. Perhaps it was on a blind date in college. Or last weekend, when you dragged your spouse along to one of your favorite activities and sensed his or her resentment. I remember the time I got a sitter for our two preschoolers and dragged Dave to a lecture about the secrets of having a successful marriage. Normally the topic would have been of interest to him; but since he was there under duress, the presentation left him cold. My coercion produced the opposite effect of mutuality.

The fact is, power plays, coercion, and manipulation destroy the potential for mutuality in a marriage. Over time the spouse who is being manipulated or coerced begins to question not just the relationship but also his or her own personal worth and identity. Such a lack of mutual love and respect sabotages any chance for a healthy love life.

Of course, mutuality doesn't mean you won't ever want a little time alone. It doesn't mean you won't ever feel like telling your partner to take a hike. All relationships experience these normal ebbs and flows. But in a mutual relationship, partners generally like being together!

Think about how good it feels when your spouse lets you know he or she wants to be with you by a gentle caress of the hand, a twinkle in the eye, or a loving comment. This quiet, mutual understanding naturally breeds security, confidence, and romance. Don't just assume your mate knows that you are glad to be married to him or her; regularly find ways to say so, verbally and nonverbally. For example:

- Give your mate a long-stemmed rose.
- Frame a picture of the two of you.
- Write a love note in the steam on the bathroom mirror.
- Say, "Go for it. I know you can do it!"
- Send a love letter, e-mail, or fax.
- Hug for ten seconds.
- Give your mate a sincere compliment in the company of his or her friends.
- Take a hike—together!

Make a habit of expressing your love in these ways and others. It will foster mutuality and help both of you feel more confident and secure in your love life.

Honesty: Communicating Your True Feelings

Honesty is as necessary to a healthy relationship as sunlight is to flowers and trees. You and your spouse must be able to relate your feelings, needs, and desires to each other truthfully and without manipulation if you want your love life to bloom and grow.

This kind of communication doesn't come naturally, however. It's an acquired skill. Most husbands and wives develop the ability to talk openly and honestly with each other about some things—work schedules, dinner menus, kids' bedtimes. But applying frankness to intimate subjects can be much harder. It takes vulnerability, commitment, and practice. (In chapter 4, we'll give you tips on communicating openly and honestly about your love life.)

The good news is, learning to be open and honest has great rewards. For one thing, you and your spouse won't have to spend a lot of unproductive time doubting and misunderstanding one another. For two, that leaves more time for love! King Solomon sums it up well in Proverbs 24:26: "An honest answer is like a kiss on the lips."

Bad Habits Are for Breaking!

Spend some time really listening to how you and your mate communicate. What negative patterns (such as taunting, nagging, or dominating) do you notice that might be barriers to more intimate and vulnerable communication? Make a mental note of your own bad habits—write them down and keep them in your wallet if you need to!—and try to eliminate them from your conversations. A greater civility will result, as well as a greater potential for true intimacy.

—Dave & Claudia

Intimacy: Becoming Soul Mates

Intimacy is the desire to know and be known. Based on trust, freely entered into by both partners, and fueled by honesty, it's that intangible quality of unity, understanding, and synergy that moves two people from being acquaintances or friends to being lovers and soul mates. It's the primary factor in their relationship that encourages them to share their dreams, needs, fears, and longings with one another.

Like all the components of a healthy love life, intimacy can ebb and flow over the life of a marriage. Maintaining a healthy level of intimacy requires time and effort. But it's time and effort well-spent!

If your level of intimacy is low, you and your partner will not feel motivated to communicate on anything more than a superficial level; physical contact will be perfunctory, if not completely nonexistent; and marital satisfaction and joy will be lacking. If your level of intimacy is high, however, you will both laugh a little more and a little louder; enjoy touching each other and being touched; feel understood and accepted; and generally feel more secure in all aspects of your life.

To begin to increase your intimacy level, ask yourself these questions:

- What are some of the ways I would like to know my spouse more intimately?
- What are some of the ways I would like my spouse to know me more intimately?

Pleasure: Giving Joy and Comfort to Each Other

While pleasure is not the sole purpose of marriage, it's certainly an important part. A comforting cup of coffee regularly shared over the Saturday paper; a much-needed, one-minute shoulder rub; a hearty laugh shared over a joke; a spontaneous kiss—all of these are pleasurable experiences that contribute to a vibrant love life.

Many times, however, the tedium of everyday life creeps in and fills up spaces that should be reserved for laughter, fun, and pleasure. Parents in particular can get weighed down by the constant fatigue, continual interruptions, lack of privacy, and lack of free time that goes with the territory of parenthood. But when a relationship loses its spark and joy, it loses much of its purpose and grounding too. You're left wondering why you're in the relationship at all.

Our active parenting years are behind us, but we still have to struggle to keep the fun in our marriage. In our empty nest, our "baby" is our work. We really enjoy working together, but we have to be on guard. We don't want our work to become our primary source of happiness. You'd think that giving each other pleasure and having fun together would be the most natural thing in the world, but it isn't. It takes work—still.

So be intentional! Pull out your calendar and make plans for romantic moments and fun times. If you're short on ideas, don't worry. We've included many ideas throughout this book to get you started. We're certain that after you've practiced the fine art of pleasure and fun for a while, your own creativity will flourish.

Sex: Joining Together Physically

The culmination of a great love life is sex. Sex is intended for procreation, but it's also intended for pleasure. It's an expression of love—the most intense and intimate experience a couple can share.

In their book *The Good Marriage,* Judith Wallerstein and Sandra Blakeslee emphasize the importance of sex by stating:

> It is very important for all couples to find ways to protect their privacy, to cherish their sexual relationship, and to guard it fiercely. A richly rewarding and stable sex life is not just a fringe benefit; it is the central task of marriage. In a good marriage, sex and love are inseparable. Sex serves a very serious function in maintaining both the quality and stability of the relationship, replenishing emotional reserves, and strengthening the marital bond.[1]

Building or rebuilding a great sex life is not a selfish physical desire; it's a necessary step toward growing and solidifying your marriage for a lifetime. Thousands of years ago, Solomon, the writer of the book of Proverbs, encouraged spouses to indulge in sexual pleasure: let "your fountain be blessed, and rejoice with the wife of your youth. As a loving deer and a graceful doe, let her breasts satisfy you at all times; and always be enraptured with her love" (Proverbs 5:18–19 NKJV). That sounds erotic to us! King Solomon's own wonderful love story is found in the Song of Songs. Why not set aside a little private time to read some of his love poems aloud with your spouse?

Take Your Vitamins!

A creative, enjoyable, satisfying love life is not a marital add-on. Far from it! It's a key to a healthy marriage. So give yourself permission to prioritize your love relationship. Keep it safe. Nurture it. Think of trust, mutuality, honesty, intimacy, pleasure, and sex as essential vitamins that will strengthen your marriage. Take them regularly—and watch your love life bloom and grow.

chapter
3

revive us again!

Are you overwhelmed? Take this quiz and find out:

Answer true or false. Give yourself one point for each false answer.

_____ *Your ultimate sexual fantasy is eight hours of uninterrupted sleep.*

_____ *Getting "turned on" means setting the baby monitor.*

_____ *You just did another all-nighter—with your child, not your spouse.*

You're celebrating your anniversary at a great restaurant. During the main course:

_____ *You fall asleep.*

_____ *You cut your partner's meat.*

_____ *Your cell phone rings—it's the sitter. Little Johnny locked her out of the house!*

_____ *Your cell phone rings—it's a client with an urgent need that won't wait.*

_____ *You're finally home and alone at last. Your partner approaches you with loving caresses—and that's the last thing you remember. Zzzzzz!*

Scoring:

6–8 *Wow! How did you do it? We're overwhelmed with your success!*

4–5 *You're on the right track—not completely overwhelmed.*

0–3 *You are definitely overwhelmed!*

Whatever your score, if you're married and breathing, you probably feel overwhelmed at times. We all do. The problem is, ongoing anxiety, pressure, and stress can sabotage a love relationship. But we have good news. You can find relief, if you're willing to work at reviving your love life.

Stop right now, take a deep breath, and remember a time when you felt *most* competent and capable. Perhaps it was when you completed a project at work, or when you success-fully pulled off your first dinner party. Maybe it was back when you ran a student organization in college, or when you built a float for your high-school homecoming parade. Now tell yourself that you can feel *that good* about your marriage and your love life. You can harness the energy, enthusiasm, and creativity that you applied back then and use it now to build the kind of love life you want.

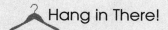

Hang in There!

We have noticed as we have been married longer, trusted each other more, and known each other better, sex has gotten better. My husband just commented a few weeks ago, "Every time we have sex, I don't think it could possibly be better than the last time, and it amazes me that it is!" That is a wonderful benefit of persevering!

—Survey Participant

Learning and Changing

You'll need that energy, enthusiasm, and creativity, too, because reviving your love life will require change. And change is never easy. Still, everyone can learn and change. Depending on personalities and learning styles, people initiate changes in their lives in one of three ways: by changing their attitude, by acquiring knowledge, or by taking action. Let's take a closer look at each of these.

Changing Your Attitude

Some people change by first changing their *attitude*. If you're this type, you need to say to yourself, "Starting today, my spouse will be first in my life! I choose to do all I can to develop a more creative love life." Your attitude adjustment will then motivate you to take action.

When our boys were young, I often felt so zapped of energy that I had very little desire for sex. I knew how important our sex life was to Dave, however, so I decided to work on changing my attitude. (Actually, our love life was important to me too—I was just so tired, I didn't know it!) I'm a thinker, and as the old proverb goes, "As a man thinks in his heart, so is he." I found that as I made the effort to think in my heart about loving Dave, I became more interested, even in my exhausted state. When I approached Dave with the attitude of wanting to meet his needs, most of the time my own interest was aroused.

Acquiring Knowledge

Other people initiate change by gaining *knowledge*. If that's you, maybe reading this book will motivate you to make your love life a high priority!

I am this type. I have a thirst for knowledge, and this has been a key in keeping my love life with Claudia strong. When we were first married, I realized that both of us had a lot to learn. I also realized that I could take the lead in scouring resources for building a creative love life. The knowledge I gained benefited us greatly, especially after the children started arriving. Claudia was often too exhausted to be creative, while I always had some energy left for sex. (Claudia called it my

"Eveready battery.") Because I had done a little research, I understood what she was going through. I also realized that we had to do more planning, scheduling, and compromising to keep our sex life afloat during the active parenting season.

Taking Action

Still other people initiate change through doing—by taking *action*. If you're an "action" person, you need to initiate change by taking that step of faith and planning a date or romantic getaway with your spouse. Don't wait until your attitude is just right or you've read every marriage book you can get your hands on. Take the Nike approach and "Just do it!" You'll be glad you did. As one participant at a Marriage Alive seminar told us, "The greatest help you gave us was raising our 'faith level.' You convinced us that we could take one little step to improve our love life. We did it, and that encouraged us to take another. Before long, our attitude changed from one of despair to hope. Thanks!"

What Changes?

What specifically do *you* need to change in order to revive your love relationship with your spouse? Only you can answer that question. But we encourage you to begin by taking inventory of your strengths and weaknesses, both individually and as a couple.

First, identify your strengths. Everyone has some! For

example, are you totally committed to your partner? Are you able to laugh rather than cry when things stack up and spin out of control? Are you an encourager? Do you see the glass half-full instead of half-empty? If you focus on your strengths, your relationship will run more smoothly. You'll spend less time trying to understand each other and have more time to invest in your love life.

Next, consider your weak areas. What factors are keeping you from having the time you need for giving and getting the love you want? How good are you at solving problems together? Do you find yourself embroiled in time-consuming, nonconstructive disagreements? Do you lack clear goals? What is your major focus in life? Are your priorities misplaced? Are you so overcommitted that when something unexpected comes along—car trouble, plumbing problems, the flu—your relationship becomes even more stressed out? No wonder you're out of emotional energy. You need to be revived! The good news is, once you've identified your weaknesses, you can begin to change them.

Four Tips for Change

Your weaknesses may not be the same as ours. We may need to change in certain areas that you don't, and vice versa. But some issues in marriage seem to be universal. We've come up with four tips for change that apply to virtually all married couples who want to revive their love life.

Tip One: Focus on Your Relationship

Face it. You can't do everything. Something has to fall through the cracks. Together you and your spouse can decide what that should be—and please, oh please, let it be something other than your love life!

It's easy to be so focused on other things—work, children, hobbies, TV, the Internet—that you forget to focus on your partner and your own personal needs. And where does that leave your love life? Certainly not as a high priority. So the first step to reviving your love life is to give yourself permission to refocus your attention on your relationship. Putting your marriage first will help you put everything else in its proper place. It will help you put life's little conflicts and trials in perspective.

Recommit yourself to your marriage. Acknowledge that it is worth investing in and cherishing. Then be alert each day to little ways you can make your marriage a higher priority. Nurture your relationship by spending time alone with your spouse. And if you start to feel guilty about taking time away from others (that is to say, your children) in order to concentrate on improving your love life, banish the thought! They, too, will benefit from your renewed focus.

Tip Two: Take Care of Yourself

For us, nothing zaps our love life like a backache. And backaches are a direct result of not taking care of ourselves. Gone are the days when we could abuse our backs without painful consequences. Now our backs are our pacers; they signal when we need to slow down and give ourselves some extra care.

What is your pacer? Stress and tension seem to seek out the weakest part of a person's anatomy. Maybe your back is healthy, but you get chronic sinusitis, allergies, or migraine headaches. Or maybe you have frequent heartburn or stomach problems. If you want to revitalize your love life, you're going to have to learn how to pace yourself and take care of your body. Without guilt, consider ways that you can be good to yourself. Here are a few ideas to get you started:

- Take fifteen minutes to sit, read, and reflect.
- Get eight hours of sleep—even if you have to catch a nap before dinner or on your lunch break.
- Hire a sitter and do whatever you want for a couple of hours.
- Take a long, relaxing bath after you put the kids in bed.
- Take a short walk.
- Exercise for fifteen minutes.
- Watch your favorite video.
- Browse through a bookstore.
- Give yourself a manicure.
- Get your hair cut.

- Call a friend and visit for fifteen minutes.

- Buy your favorite candy bar and share it with your spouse.

Tip Three: Take Care of Your Marriage

Taking care of yourself gives you the energy you need to take care of your marriage. Taking care of your marriage means taking care of your spouse—putting him or her first on your priority list. If you have kids, your children may require more actual time; but your partner must be your first priority if you want to have a healthy home and a healthy love life.

We like what one survey participant wrote: "When I walk in the door, the first thing I do is hug my spouse. The kids are next, but I think it's healthy for our children to see in practical ways how we put our love first." Another wife told us, "I may spend hours supervising homework assignments and carting kids here and there, but each evening our children know that for fifteen minutes their dad and I are not available to them—that's our time to focus on each other. They can't interrupt us unless the house is on fire!"

These two are on the right track, because nothing chal-lenges marital intimacy more than parenthood. (If you don't have kids, recognize that your career may be your "baby.") Balancing the roles of partner and parent is one of the most difficult tasks a couple can face. As one mom wrote, "Before kids, our lovemaking was great. Now I'm too tired with caregiving, keeping everything on track at home, and managing a part-time job. I'm just so dormant. Is this normal? My husband is still interested, but I'm not. To be honest, I don't really want to find time for sex."

Our answer to her: Find time anyway! In his book *Super Marital Sex*, Paul Pearsall notes that "as many marriages fail because of children as children fail because of faulty marriages. Until we learn that children are not special, but equal in importance to all of us, until we learn that we must not lead

Let Your Marriage Be Center Stage

Late nights with sick children leave me burned out to the point of exhaustion. I find myself exhausted emotionally, mentally, and physically. But I have a loving, sensitive husband who cares for me and helps out around the house and with the children. It's so important that burdens are shared equally so that one of us doesn't get crazy! My advice is: Your kids need to know that they are not the center of your marriage and that you have other priorities besides them. They need to see a healthy, loving relationship between their parents. Take advantage of baby-sitting—an exchange program with other couples, if necessary. When we can, we try to be romantic, spontaneous, and creative; and we always carry a condom!

—Survey Participant

our lives and marriages for children but with them, we sacrifice our marriages and our own development."[1]

"That sounds great," one seminar participant responded when we shared that quote. "But I feel guilty when I don't put my children first. If I'm making my husband my priority, then I'm letting other things, like my parenting role, slip."

Guilt is a universal feeling. We all experience it from time to time. But Ellen Kreidman, in her book *Is There Sex after Kids?* says that mothers experience guilt much more frequently and more intensely than fathers. "Guilt is an inherited disease," she writes, "one passed down from mother to daughter, generation after generation. I have found that women, especially mothers, feel guilty no matter what they do. If they stay home and bake cookies, they feel guilty because they aren't 'fulfilling' themselves with a challenging career or contributing to the family coffers. If they work full time, they feel guilty because they aren't fully involved with their children. . . . And working part time is sometimes the greatest guilt inducer of all—leaving a mother feeling bad for giving only half an effort to the kids and half an effort to her job."[2]

Whether we like it or not, the major responsibilities in the home fall mostly to the mother. But today a majority of mothers work, leaving them with less time than women of past generations for the rest of life—and specifically for homemaking. With what amounts to two full-time jobs, a mom can easily feel overwhelmed and guilty, especially if she picked up high homemaking expectations from *her* mother (who most likely didn't work outside the home).

"In my home growing up," one woman said, "my mom was a great homemaker. You could eat off the floor. You can eat off the floor in my house, too—Cheerios, SpaghettiOs, Teddy Grahams, and animal crackers!"

The reality is, working mothers have two large chunks of time already spoken for: job and kids. There is little discretionary time left over. But at least there's some! And discretionary time is just that—you choose how you want to invest it. Wise couples choose to invest some of their discretionary time in making their marriage a priority. (In chapter 6 we'll look more closely at the time issue and help you free up minutes you didn't know you had.)

Even if you only have a few extra minutes each day, you can invest them in your marriage. For example, you can:

- Call your honey and say "I love you because . . ."

- Scratch your lover's back.

- Get up with the baby in the middle of the night and let your spouse sleep.

- Let voice mail collect your calls or turn the phone ringer off for a few minutes and focus on your mate.

- Put on your spouse's favorite music.

- Light a scented candle in the bedroom.

- Eat a bowl of ice cream together after the kids are in bed.

- Write a letter that tells your mate why you would marry him or her all over again.
- Write love messages on Post-it notes and stick them where your spouse is sure to see them.

Tip Four: Let Your Marriage Be Good to Your Children

If you're a parent, then you need to be aware that your love life can influence your children in a positive way. When children grow up in happy, intact, functional families with parents who love each other, they unconsciously learn the positive roles they will later play in marriage and parenthood. In other words, as you focus on your marriage, you mentor your own children!

Consider three ways your own healthy marriage can benefit your children:

1. Your Marriage Provides Stability

A strong marriage significantly enhances children's security and stability by letting them know that the unconditional, lifelong love they see modeled between their parents also applies to them. Typically, children first experience God's love through their parents. Even seeing their parents arguing and then making up demonstrates to them that life goes on, and love is not diminished in the face of disagreements and stress.

"We don't try to hide our disagreements from our children," one mother told us. "They need to know that we can disagree, but we still love each other and are totally committed to our marriage and family. In my home I never heard my parents disagree. Then one day, when I was thirteen, my dad just left. I didn't know anything was amiss. It was devastating! Life just isn't like that.

"My husband says that if we agreed on everything, life would be boring. So one way we mentor our children is by modeling positive ways to resolve conflict. But we also laugh and have fun together as a couple and as a family."

2. *Your Marriage Sets the Tone*

The way you and your spouse relate to each other sets the atmosphere in your home. If you habitually joke and laugh together, your home will be a fun place to be; and your children will learn how to laugh and enjoy life. Conversely, if your kids only see you arguing, they are likely to grow up being argumentative themselves. They'll assume that arguing is the normal way people interact with each other.

A healthy atmosphere includes a healthy balance of both confrontation and laughter. When our children were young, I was the resident worrier, while Dave was the family jokester. Together over the years we learned how to strike the right balance between us. We learned that there are times for joking, and there are times to express serious concerns. But whether joking or serious, we always tried to be real and have no hidden undertones in our conversations. Nothing is worse than a home where words are polite but underneath is

40

hostility, bitterness, and tension so thick you can cut it with a knife.

3. Your Marriage Helps Shape Relationships

Think about your own parents and what you observed while you were growing up. What did they model for you? Were they loving and affectionate with each other? Huggers usually come from families of huggers. You have probably picked up many of the ways of relating that were taught to you (consciously or not) by your parents.

The upside to this is that if you work to build a strong, loving marriage, your children will learn how to give and receive love, how to nurture, how to resolve conflict, how to communicate, and how to live—by watching you. Loving behaviors will be as natural to them as breathing and will be the foundation for all their future relationships. What a legacy to give to your kids!

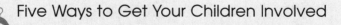

Five Ways to Get Your Children Involved

1. Let your kids help you plan a surprise for Mom or Dad.
2. Have a family hug.
3. Tell your children ten reasons you love your spouse.
4. Get your kids to help you plan a romantic date.
5. Talk with your children about what they want in a future mate.

—Dave & Claudia

Take our tips. Make time for yourself and for your marriage. Focus on reviving and nurturing your love life. Remember, parenting is a temporary job. Your kids will be out of the house in about eighteen years, but your mate is there for life! Someday your children (and their spouses) will thank you for the great role model you set for them—and you'll have a vibrant, still-growing love life to give you joy and fulfillment in your empty nest years.

part
2

in just a few minutes...

you can learn how to build
a creative love life!

chapter 4

building blocks for great sex

"Having my own home-based editorial business sounded so clever," a woman named Abby told us. "What insanity to think I could balance life, love, and the pursuit of *anything!* I don't even have time to go to the bathroom alone."

As we talked, Abby's three-year-old daughter, Olivia, played at our feet, stacking blocks on top of blocks. Then, almost as if to illustrate her mother's point, Olivia kicked the blocks at the foundation; and the wobbly structure crashed to the floor.

"That's exactly how I feel," Abby exclaimed. "My life is like a pile of blocks stacked precariously on top of each other. One false move, and everything will come crashing down!"

Can you identify with Abby? Do you feel as if your life is spinning out of control? Why is it so hard to balance everything you have to do? Managing life in a traditional family is difficult enough; but if you happen to be living in a blended family and a second or third marriage, your task is even more complicated. You have more blocks to balance.

What are the building blocks for your marriage? For your love life? Is the structure a little wobbly? Perhaps it's time for a building inspection—time to make sure the foundational blocks of your relationship are solidly in place. We've identified five building blocks that are crucial: communication, conflict resolution, encouragement, shared core beliefs, and commitment to growth. Let's look at each of these individually.

Building Block #1: Communication
"We Need to Talk!"

One survey participant said, "To me, sex is just one more thing to do—something else that somebody needs from me. Once I get into it, I'm okay, but it takes a lot of mental preparation. I'm always thinking about what I have to do when I'm done. It would help if my husband would spend time just talking to me at other times!"

The fact is, communication is the most fundamental building block in any relationship. When you have difficulty communicating with your partner, you either spend hours talking about issues and trying to get to a basic understanding of what each other thinks, or you don't make the effort to talk at all. By sharpening your communication skills, you can avoid misunderstandings and hurt feelings and find more time for your love life.

In our survey we discovered that it's possible to have good communication and a lousy sex life, but it's next to impossible to have a great sex life and lousy communication. Communication is foundational to great sex. Nearly every couple that reported having a great love life also reported communicating well with one another. And those couples that said they have good marital communication reported more satisfaction with their sexual relationship.

That's because, in large part, communicative couples find it easier than noncommunicative ones to talk about their love lives. If you don't talk with your partner about your sexual relationship, you're missing out on a whole dimension of loving. As one of our psychologist friends told us, "If you don't talk, think, or read about sex, you'll soon forget about it!"

How can you begin to talk about your love life? We have three tips:

1. Listen for Feelings

There is no time more important to listen for feelings than when you talk about sex. "Honey, I've got a headache," is a phrase that can be intended to convey many different messages. It may mean exactly what it says: "I have a headache." Or it could mean:

- "You ignored me this morning, so I'm going to ignore you now."
- "I just don't have the energy for or interest in sex right now."

- "Why can't you start with romance? Then I might be more interested in sex."
- "I need some time to myself before I can focus on anyone else."

Understanding the hidden emotional messages behind words is difficult. (Of course, sometimes there are no hidden messages—and we still get stumped!) As you listen for your spouse's feelings, observe his or her countenance and body language, including posture, gestures, and glances. Mixed in with the nonverbal communication may be that "Come hither" look that tells you, "I'm in the mood for love!" That love

How Do You Really Feel?

Men and women often communicate differently, and sometimes it's hard for us to hear and understand each other's emotions. One of the hardest things for me to do when I'm listening to Dave is to refrain from making assumptions about what he's thinking or feeling. My advice to wives? Be observant, but don't read too much into your husband's nonverbal cues. Before any serious conversation, agree to take each other's words at face value. When you think your husband's nonverbal communication may be contradicting his words, gently say to him, "Tell me again how you really feel about this." Then really listen! You may be amazed at what you hear.

—Claudia

potential may simply remain potential, however, unless you take our next tip.

2. Talk about Sex

"My husband, Keith, just doesn't understand what turns me on," Mindy confided to us in one of our Marriage Alive seminars. "He's too rough. It's like he goes for the kill without giving me time to get into lovemaking."

"Do you talk about your lovemaking?" we asked her. "Do you tell him how you would like for him to approach you?"

"Oh no," Mindy replied. "We never talk about it. We just do it."

The "just doing it" was not satisfying for Mindy. And the truth was, it wasn't satisfying for Keith either. They desperately needed to talk to each other.

Unfortunately, Mindy and Keith's situation is not unique. Many couples don't talk about sex. If you are simply assuming that you know what your partner wants and how he or she feels, we have news for you: you're probably wrong. And the bedroom isn't a great place for guesswork.

Why do people who can talk for hours about their jobs, hobbies, and children find sex such an embarrassing, touchy (pardon the pun) topic? Maybe they tried to talk about sex once, but they ended up criticizing or blaming each other and hurting one another's feelings. (For men in particular, self-esteem is often tied to sexual performance.) Or, maybe they want to talk about sex but just don't have the vocabulary.

These obstacles can be overcome. Just a few simple communication skills can help you talk openly and honestly about your sex life without blaming or attacking your partner. For instance, start your sentences with "I" and let them reflect back on you as the speaker. Mindy could have said, "Honey, I need you to touch me tenderly before I can respond sexually. Hugs, kisses, and even telling me how much you love me throughout the day help me open up and respond to you."

The message Keith would receive from such a statement would be quite different from the message he'd get from "You're too rough and hurry too much" or "You aren't trying to please me at all!" or "Why can't you be gentler?"

Avoiding "you" statements, "why" questions, and the words *never* and *always* will help keep the conversation positive and productive. So will the generous use of *please* and *thank you.*

3. Develop Your Own Vocabulary

While nonverbal communication such as hugs and kisses are an important part of any love language, you also need words. Remember, your mate is not a mind reader! If you rely only on nonverbal cues, we guarantee you will misread each other. Instead, you need to develop your own sex vocabulary. It's like learning to speak a new language—only this time you get to decide the meaning of the words.

Early in our marriage, before we had children, we had a parakeet named Chirpy. One evening we were at our neighbors' home and noticed that it was getting late. All day long we had been sending each other love signals. We wanted to head home, so to initiate our departure Dave said, "We need to go home now. It's time to feed Chirpy." Our friends saw right through us and laughed us out the door. Since then, from time to time we referred to making love as "feeding Chirpy." Now, years later, we still talk about "feeding the birds," as in: "Honey, don't you think it's time to feed the birds?" "What about meeting for lunch and feeding the birds?" It's our private love vocabulary!

King Solomon understood the importance of having a love vocabulary. Three thousand years ago he coined this love language in the Song of Songs:

"Your eyes are doves."

"He browses among the lilies."

"Your lips are like a scarlet ribbon."

"Your two breasts are like two fawns, like twin fawns of a gazelle."

"Your lips drop sweetness as the honeycomb; . . . milk and honey are under your tongue."

"You are a garden fountain, a well of flowing water."

"Let my lover come into his garden and taste its choice fruits."

"His body is like polished ivory decorated with sapphires."

"His mouth is sweetness itself; he is altogether lovely."[1]

We can all take some tips from King Solomon. Other sources can help us develop our love talk too. Poetry and music, for example, can add to our love vocabulary. So can reading books. One survey participant shared: "My husband and I read the book *Mars and Venus in the Bedroom* by John Gray together. Everything in the book wasn't for us; but it had some wonderful insights, and we learned a lot about each other's physical and emotional needs. We'd read a chapter, then go to bed. (By the way, this was my husband's idea!)"

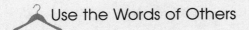

Use the Words of Others

As you're reading books about love and marriage, highlight those passages that express your feelings. Then write in the margin: "Yes! That's me" or "Ditto." Using someone else's words to communicate your feelings and needs will eventually give you the confidence to form your own.

—Dave & Claudia

Building Block #2: Conflict Resolution
"We Need to Work It Out!"

One seminar participant asked us, "What if we start talking about sex, and we find that we disagree? What do we do?"

"You keep talking," we told him.

That leads us to our next building block for a great love life: learning to solve problems together. This will be easier if we follow the good advice in James 1:19 to be "quick to listen, slow to speak, and slow to become angry." In many marriages too much precious "love time" is lost in fruitless and unproductive arguments. How much time could *you* free up by taking just a few minutes to work on your conflict resolution skills? These critical abilities will help you whenever you disagree—even when the disagreement is about sex.

We guarantee your efforts will pay off. According to our survey, couples who have difficulty resolving conflict—just like those who have difficulty communicating—usually experience low sexual satisfaction. When they are skilled at handling conflict, however, they tend to have a great sexual relationship.

Both of us are strong-willed, opinionated people. At times we totally disagree with each other—even about our sex life. At times we misunderstand each other and get angry. But we try not to stay angry. Years ago, marriage enrichment pioneers David and Vera Mace taught us how to make an "anger contract" that we try to put into immediate effect whenever either of us becomes angry. We can't tell you how much time we

---

Our Anger Contract

1. We agree to tell each other when we are getting angry.

2. We agree not to vent our anger at each other.

3. We agree to ask for the other's help in solving whatever is causing the anger.

Signed: _____

Signed: _____ [2]

---

have saved by using this contract to short-circuit unproductive arguments! Basically, the contract looks like this:

Why not make your own anger-contract with your spouse? It may turn out to be one of the best things you ever do for your love life! We also recommend two great books that deal extensively with anger management and conflict resolution in marriage: *Love and Anger in Marriage* by David Mace[3] and *Fighting for Your Marriage* by Howard Markman, Scott Stanley, and Susan Blumberg.[4]

Of course, relationships are fluid, and most couples are still in the process of developing effective methods for coping with anger, problems, and conflict. That's okay. Your relationship with your spouse is a journey, not a destination. You don't suddenly arrive at a great marriage and a great sex life. But wherever you are along the road, you *can* move forward.

As one survey participant wrote: "It's often hard to remember that today is not the last day on earth we have to get it right, so we often go to bed feeling as if things will never improve. Nothing drives healthy sexual intimacy further away than feelings of inadequacy. That is why we have to keep reminding each other to let the law of love be uppermost and to forgive each other for our shortcomings. By God's grace, there is always tomorrow to begin anew; and if we don't allow failure to saturate our souls, we can keep growing and find our lovemaking to be a source of great strength and bonding."

Wise advice! Forgiving and accepting each other paves the

way for a closer, more intimate love life and moves us to the next building block.

Building Block #3: Encouragement
"We Need to Build Each Other Up!"

The third basic building block is encouragement. How are you doing at building up your partner? When was the last time you complimented your spouse on being a great lover? When was the last time you sent an e-mail with an encouragement in the subject line, left a supportive voice message on the answering machine, or tacked a love note on the refrigerator? Positive patterns, consistently practiced, become positive habits!

One wife asked in a seminar, "What do you mean by encouragement? If I encouraged my husband, I'd never get out of bed! How do you encourage a mate who is always ready?"

Encouragement has two aspects. First, as a foundation to your relationship, encouragement involves establishing patterns of support and praise that affirm your mate's identity and worth. Second, as a foundation for your love life, encouragement involves affirming and initiating sexual intimacy.

Establishing Patterns of Support and Praise

Everyone needs to feel loved and valued—including your spouse. Did you know that in terms of a person's psyche and self-esteem, it takes five positive statements to offset the impact of one negative statement?[5] Listen for twenty-four hours to how you talk to your mate and see what your ratio is. Then determine to develop the habit of affirmation and encouragement by taking a few minutes each day to give your spouse an honest compliment or two.

The truth is, we often take for granted the little things our spouses do that enhance our relationships and strengthen our families. By recognizing these things and speaking words of praise, you can instantly build up your mate's sense of self-esteem and contentment—and your love life. Start by making a list of different aspects about your mate that you can encourage and affirm. Some of these may include:

- Working hard in a job or profession
- Parenting well
- Being attractive
- Maintaining or achieving physical fitness
- Staying intellectually sharp
- Maintaining social obligations
- Managing finances
- Growing spiritually
- Homemaking with creativity
- Having a good sense of humor and the ability to laugh

Affirming and Initiating Sexual Intimacy

Often a husband and wife's sex drives and expectations are different. One may be "high desire" and the other "low desire."

One therapist told us that half his clients complain that their mates bother them all the time to have sex, and the other half complain that their mates never bother them. "If only I could shuffle the couples, everyone would be happy!" he said.

Because of these differences, being able to communicate with your partner about your sexual needs is critical. In the process you may need to encourage a spirit of adventure and a willingness to explore together. If you want your spouse to try something different or do something more frequently, for example, you may need to give gentle encouragement—and not just in the bedroom. Encouragement toward intimacy can take place all day long. A smile, a kiss, a certain look across the room, a phone call, an unexpected "I love you" note—all of these can go far in paving the way toward sexual intimacy.

Even if you're short on time, you can find little ways to express encouragement to your mate. For example, you can get great deals on Valentine cards on February 15. Why not stock up and send or hide Valentine cards throughout the year? You can add your own intimate message. When we were first married, we used to make greeting cards for each other. In them we'd let each other know what recent sexual experiences we particularly enjoyed and what we were looking forward to.

Here's another great tip we got from a survey participant: Note something specific that your mate does to encourage you. Wait two or three weeks, and then take a couple of minutes to encourage him or her in the same way. Or try this: Create your own "Deck of Love." Write out cards that tell your spouse how you would like to be encouraged. For example, I like it when you . . .

- Rub my back at night

- Offer to put the kids to bed or clean the kitchen

- Shave on your day off

- Whisper in my ear that you love me

- Hold my hand

- Call me for no reason

Keep your cards in an obvious, convenient place. Choose one each day and place it where your spouse can see it as a "memory jogger." Whatever you do, we're convinced that spouses cannot give each other too much genuine encouragement. Encouragement is like a marital vitamin; taken daily, it adds energy and joy to your love life.

Building Block #4: Core Belief System
"We Need Spiritual Intimacy!"

The fourth building block is spiritual intimacy, which involves sharing core beliefs and making time for your faith. But time, as we've noted, can be hard to come by. One clever, time-challenged couple bought two copies of the same devotional book and separately read through it. The husband kept his copy at his office, and the wife kept her copy in the bathroom. When they had a few minutes together, they talked about the devotion they each had read separately. Instead of being discouraged that they couldn't read their devotions together, they accepted reality and came up with a new strategy for connecting spiritually.

Perhaps you don't consider yourself "spiritually inclined." You're not alone. Many people don't think about their spiritual lives until they're in a crisis or going through a significant transition. Before becoming parents we never paid much attention to our spiritual lives or our core beliefs. Then a difficult birth and a baby who didn't immediately breathe launched our spiritual search. We realized that we needed more than just sexual intimacy. We needed a spiritual intimacy that would add depth to our relationship, hold us together through the storms of life, and give us a purpose for living that was greater than the two—now three—of us.

We also realized that our faith in God and the values and morals we held—our belief system—affected our sexual relationship. Dr. Pearsall, in *Super Marital Sex*, reports that "belief systems are as important, perhaps more important, to sexuality as any other area of life. Developing a shared belief system is central to super marital sex. This is why marriage offers a unique opportunity for intimacy, for it provides the time and opportunity for spiritual growth through life changes."[6]

This should not surprise us. God is the one who created men and women as sexual beings. He is the originator of sex. He created us with the capacity for great sexual pleasure. And the fact is, those couples whose marriages have a spiritual dimension are often the most fulfilled sexually. Sociologist Andrew Greeley surveyed married people and found that couples who frequently pray together are twice as likely as those who pray less often to describe their marriages as being highly romantic. They also report considerably higher sexual satisfaction.[7]

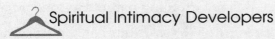 Spiritual Intimacy Developers

1. Praying together
2. Worshiping together
3. Reading the Bible together
4. Reading a devotional book together
5. Taking a class together at church
6. Forgiving each other

—Dave & Claudia

For us, spiritual intimacy has contributed greatly to our marriage and our love life. We began by developing spiritual intimacy with God first and then taking a few minutes each day to pray together. This spiritual closeness has helped us open up to each other and share our most private hopes and fears in all areas of our lives. Our faith directly influences our love life, giving it a spiritual dimension. As Greeley notes, sexual union is actually part of the sacrament of marriage.[8] In our core belief system, we consider sex to be a sacred trust given for our mutual pleasure. It is part of the glue that holds us together.

Building Block #5: Commitment to Growth
"We Need to Nurture Our Love!"

The last building block for great sex is being committed to growing together and nurturing your love for each other. Sometimes that requires being willing to sacrifice for one another. Take Alexia and Carter, for example. Alexia had always wanted to take art lessons, but as a busy mother of three, she just didn't have the time. Imagine her glee when her husband surprised her by registering her for a six-week art class at a local gallery. He also agreed to come home early on Tuesday evenings so he could be there with the kids while she attended the class. As Carter quickly discovered, sacrificial love and a commitment to your partner's personal growth leads to romance!

How mindful are you of your partner's dreams and desires? Are you willing to facilitate times for his or her personal growth by sacrificing some of your own time? Are you committed to your partner's growth and to the growth of your relationship together?

Having a commitment to a growing marriage relationship is vital. Unfortunately, too many couples have reinterpreted their marriage vows, making "till death do us part" seem more like "until I'm not happy anymore." Without a commitment to permanence and growth, marriages all too easily die. For this reason, couples getting married today face a 60 percent possibility of divorce or permanent separation.[9]

How would you rate your commitment to your marriage? In what ways would you like to see your marriage grow and improve?

Begin by affirming your commitment to having a growing love life. Then work to maintain it, particularly through the parenting years. When we were raising our children, we often had to sacrifice our own time together to meet the critical needs of others. But at other times, we consciously put the needs of others on hold and took care of our marriage. We were absolutely determined to get through the rough spots, to somehow work out a solution for our differing sex drives, to make time for loving each other, and to arrive at the empty nest stage with our love life intact. Because we didn't give up during the hectic parenting years, we are finding that this is the best stage yet!

We still have to make the effort to invest in our love life, and that kind of investment is hard work—at any stage. As one wife told us, "We've been married for eleven years, and most of that time my husband has worked evenings and nights. One way we've stayed connected is that each year I buy a small, spiral-bound notebook and leave him a note before I go to bed. It only takes a couple of minutes and is really easy to do. Sometimes I let him know how my day went, a cute thing one of our three boys said or did, or bits of information, like 'I want you to wake me up to snuggle.'

"I have one rule: I don't write about an unresolved issue or something that may upset him or cause him to worry—those things are kept for open discussion. I always say 'I love you.' Over the years, he has let me know how much he appreciates the notes—especially if I happen to forget to leave one. It is something small that builds our relationship and that both of us have come to enjoy. It's also a journaling of our years together—a model perhaps for our sons to follow."

This woman has the right idea. Rather than allow obstacles and circumstances to hinder her, she has found her own special way to stay connected to her spouse and to affirm her commitment to the growth of her marriage. No, it's not easy. But she's building her love life, one block—and note—at a time.

You can too.

chapter

5

expectations: getting on the same page

Did you see the movie *Annie Hall* starring Woody Allen? In an attempt to salvage their marriage, a husband and wife make separate visits to the same marriage counselor. The wife goes in first and complains, "My husband wants to make love all the time—like three or four times each week!" The husband goes in next and tells the counselor, "My wife never wants to make love—why, we only have sex three or four times a week!"

The truth is, for the typical time-starved couple, making love three or four times a week is only a dream (or a night-mare, depending on your perspective). In fact, according to one study, 20 percent of married couples have sex fewer than ten times a year.[1] But whether sex is a monthly occurrence or something that happens every other night, it's a safe bet that most husbands and wives have different expectations about their love lives.

That's because, quite simply, men and women are different. "She" isn't a female "he," and "he" isn't a male "she." A wife may be looking for tenderness, romance, and intimacy. Her husband may want passion and quick release. He may be "high desire" and she "low desire"—or the other way around.

Understanding each other's expectations is one of the keys to having a great sex life. You and your spouse may not have the same levels of desire; but if someone asked, "Would you like to have a better love life?" you'd both probably say yes. That means you're going to have to invest time in your love life and learn how to express your expectations verbally, specifically, and realistically. It means you're going to have to get on the same page with your partner.

What Page?

Our friends Jenny and David are avid readers. When the latest historical novel hits their favorite bookstore, they're in line to pick up their copy. Being the frugal-minded couple that they are, they usually share a copy instead of buying two books. You'd think this wouldn't be a problem, since they keep very different hours. Jenny likes to read before her bedtime of 9:00 p.m., while David usually has two or three more hours to go before he ends his evening. Their problem isn't *sharing* the book; it's *talking* about it the next day. You see, they don't read at the same pace. So when Jenny comments on some aspect of the thickening plot, David cries out, "Don't tell me about that. I'm not there yet!"

Crafting a love life is much like sharing a novel. In order for it to be mutually enjoyable, you and your partner have to get on the same page. Rare are the husband and wife, however, who want the same things in a love life, the same types of pleasure, in the same quantities. More typical are two people with very different desires and expectations trying their best to come to a mutually satisfying middle ground—a process complicated by the time pressures of married life and parenting.

During a Marriage Alive seminar, one participant asked us, "How can anyone have an exciting sex life after children come along? Romance must be for people without kids."

"I know what you mean," another participant added. "With kids, you have to factor in the lack of time, energy, and privacy. It seems that on those rare occasions when I do feel amorous, my husband isn't interested; or there's a child asleep in our bed!"

"Having children doesn't mean that you can't have romance or a creative love life," we assured the group. "You just have to work harder at it. You have to talk through your expectations. You have to get on the same page."

"But what if your page is blank?" someone called out.

The group laughed, and we responded, "You have to start *somewhere*. Actually, it's not a bad idea to start with a blank page—to erase your unrealistic expectations and start fresh."

We know from experience what we're talking about! Over the years we've had to work hard to get on and stay on the same page, especially during the hectic parenting years. One thing that helped us was to establish a tradition of taking marriage getaways. We found that even twenty-four hours away together, alone, was often just the ticket for reenergizing our love life.

Sometimes our expectations for our getaways were different, however. We especially remember two getaways—but for very different reasons. On the first getaway, we went to a cabin in Alabama for a weekend. It was our first chance to be alone after becoming parents, and it was "love city" from the time we got there till the time we left. I remember the weekend, which was full of sex, as a big "10." Claudia remembers being oh so exhausted!

We spent the second getaway at the beach in Florida. Claudia fondly remembers the slow pace, the long walks on the beach, the candlelit dinners for two, the shopping together. For her, it was a great week. I remember it as a great week too, but I have to admit I was disappointed that we didn't make love every day we were there. (After all, isn't that the point of a marriage getaway?)

In Sickness and in Health

Having a love life definitely takes effort. And when things don't work out the way you've planned, you have to persevere. Take our twentieth anniversary, for example. To celebrate two decades of marriage, Dave planned a romantic get-away. He reserved the honeymoon suite, complete with a heart-shaped spa and a dozen red roses.

There we were, on the threshold of one of the most romantic anniversary settings you could imagine. But it wasn't to be.

"It's just not fair!" I said, fighting back tears. "Everything is so perfect. Why did this happen to us?"

"I know. It's a real bummer!" Dave responded. "Certainly not what I planned. But we'll have other times in the future."

Feeling little comfort, I grabbed the roses and took one last glance at the beautiful, untouched room that held such promise for romance and love. Dashed expectations! Hope deferred until who knows when! Then we closed the door, got in our car, and started the drive home to our youngest son, Jonathan, who had just come down with the flu.

Later that evening, we spent a quiet anniversary with our sick little boy. "Remember the words in our wedding liturgy, 'in sickness and in health'?" Dave asked. "Well, it should include, 'and when your kids have the flu too.'"

Sometimes our own illnesses have ruined great romantic escapes. We remember the time we got away to the House on the Metolius, our favorite romantic spot in the mountains near Sisters, Oregon, only to have Dave come down with bronchitis. He couldn't lie down without having a coughing attack. He ended up sleeping on the couch.

Simple, everyday setbacks can wipe out the best-laid plans and wreak havoc with expectations. You arrange to stay home together for a couple of hours, and the office calls with an urgent need: "You must come in right away!" Or you plan a romantic evening, and your mate falls asleep in the recliner reading the newspaper. Sometimes it's not that you're not on the same page—you aren't even reading the same book!

But I Thought . . .

Without a doubt, the most frustrating times we've experienced in our marriage have been when we've misread each other's expectations—usually because we've failed to talk about them. Even when we talk, however, and our desires are compatible, we still misunderstand each other from time to time.

We often combine writing with our travels, and we try to arrange to have blocks of time in beautiful, isolated settings. We love to get away from the phone, fax, and people. We actually wrote part of this book in the Black Forest of southern Germany. Now, as you might imagine, writing a book called *No Time for Sex* when we had all the time and energy in the world was a very pleasant experience! We were able to do a good bit of research. Yet despite the ideal circumstances, we still misread each other's expectations.

One day we were getting ready to go for a walk. I noticed that Dave had not shaved. Rather than speak up, I thought, *He thinks I'm not interested in sex today, so he doesn't care how he looks.*

Meanwhile Dave, who actually had amorous feelings, was thinking, *We'll just get hot and sweaty on our walk, so why shave now? I'll get cleaned up and shave afterward. Maybe we'll shower together, and then . . .*

My stream of thought continued: *I wish he would shave. It would be fun to stop along the way as we walk and kiss—like we did years ago when we were dating and went hiking in the Smoky Mountains. Guess he's not interested!*

At the same time Dave silently wondered, *What's bugging Claudia? She must not be interested in sex today!*

Finally, we realized that something was going on. We were on different pages! When we told each other what we had been assuming, we realized we were both wrong. Apparently, we will never outgrow our need to identify, communicate, and understand each other's expectations.

Understanding Expectations

To craft a fulfilling love life, you must know two things: what you want out of a love life and what your partner wants out of a love life. It's not as easy as you'd think to figure these out. Most of us carry around so much emotional and relational baggage that sorting out what is truly important in a love life is a confusing process. To make matters worse, many of us have a media-created image of what a love life should be. We believe the unrealistic portrayals we see all around us in movies, soap operas, magazine articles, and sensual commercials. Unfortunately, these false images are deadly to a truly satisfying, flesh-and-blood love relationship.

Why should you make the effort to identify your own needs and desires? Because identifying them and then communicating them gives your partner the opportunity to meet them. To expect your spouse to read your mind about what you want is unfair. Being a "silent partner" only sets you up for feelings of rejection and dissatisfaction, increasing the likelihood that your negative emotions will affect other areas of your marriage relationship. If, on the other hand, you take the time to sort out your needs and desires and then use the communication tools we discuss in this book to talk about them, a truly wonderful and fulfilling sex life can unfold.

Talking about your sexual expectations is definitely one of the most intimate things you will ever do with your spouse. That's why we recommend that such conversations be initiated in an atmosphere of trust, unconditional love, and acceptance. Yes, in the process you will discover that you have differences in your levels of desire and feelings of adventurousness. That's okay. Just remember these three tips as you talk: be verbal, be specific, and be realistic.

Be Verbal

It's not enough to send signals or read body language. If you want to get on the same page, you're going to have to talk with your spouse about your expectations for your love life. What are the most satisfying aspects of your love life? What obstacles do you need to overcome? Don't be surprised if you discover that you and your partner have different expectations; in fact, you should probably be surprised if they're the same! The simple act of being verbal will help you better understand each other's needs and desires.

Talk It Over

Sit down with your spouse and discuss your expectations in the following areas. Use a range from one to ten. One means, "You definitely don't understand my expectations. Let's talk." Ten means, "Wow! We're on the same page."

_____ intimacy and closeness

_____ romance

_____ sexual fulfillment

_____ adventurousness

Don't hesitate to add other topics to your list!

—Dave & Claudia

Be Specific

When identifying what you want out of your love relationship, be specific. For example:

- How often would you like to have sex?
- How much hugging and cuddling do you need before intercourse? (Put the answer in minutes if necessary.)
- Do you need romance to set the mood?

• What are the fantasies you have been secretly hoping to try?

These questions may sound a little selfish or crass, but they're important. To work toward the goal of a mutually fulfilling love life, you must know what will fulfill you and what will fulfill your spouse—specifically.

Here's What I Would Like!

Make a list of your desires and expectations. Have your spouse do the same. Then categorize your response to the items on each other's lists using this range:

1. "No way. Never!"

2. "You might be able to talk me into it."

3. "I'll bargain with you on that one."

4. "Sure, that's easy."

5. "It would be my pleasure!"

Now pull out your calendar and schedule in a month's worth of mutually agreed-upon pleasuring. (Important: use code if your kids—or worse, your parents—might see the calendar!) Do your best to stick to your schedule and plan in advance for any baby-sitting you'll need.

—Dave & Claudia

Be Realistic

Each season of marriage offers its own challenges and opportunities for growth and requires a reexamination of expectations. What is realistic in one season may be totally unrealistic in another. Here is how we see those seasons as we look back over our forty-plus years of marriage.

Early Marriage Years: Discovering How to Love Each Other

We were married when we were still in school. Balancing college, work, and a new relationship wasn't easy, but we found time for loving each other and discovering our individual sexual likes and dislikes. We found that the more we talked about our expectations, the less inhibited we were. We read books, we experimented, and we discovered what worked for us.

What was early marriage like for you? Talking about what your expectations and experiences were when you were first married will help you get on the same page now. What did you enjoy doing in your early love life that you no longer do? If you are parents, having the same level of spontaneity as you did before you had kids is not realistic; but perhaps you could include in your planned times of loving each other some things you did before the children were born.

If you're newly married, get in the talking habit now; and understand that the first years of marriage will bring many adjustments. Years ago, when marriages were arranged by parents, the culture provided time for a new husband and wife to adjust to each other. In biblical times that period lasted twelve months. A man who took a new wife was deferred from military duty and not charged with any business for one full year.

Not so today! Little help is given these days to newlyweds. Some young couples have never even witnessed a healthy, enriched marriage, because they've come from single-parent homes or homes where romantic love died long ago. Everyone needs models and mentors. Do you know an older couple that you and your spouse can talk to—a mature husband and wife who have a great marriage and love life? If not, make an effort to find a mentor couple among your family, friends, church acquaintances, or coworkers. Your love life will be all the better for it! Then when you're older and your love life is flourishing, you can return the favor and become mentors yourselves.

Baby and Toddler Years: Helping Our Love Life Survive

If you are new parents, realistic expectations may boil down to two things: maintenance and survival. As we've discussed, a baby can definitely complicate your love life. Before you know it, everything else in your life seems to come before love—the baby, your career advancement, friends, your social life. In this season, if you're not proactive, sex can become an obligation or something you just don't think about. It's vital that you and your spouse talk about your expectations and devise a workable plan.

Our own expectations in the early parenting season were different, even when it came to handling exhaustion. When I was exhausted, I was totally exhausted. No life in this gal until my battery was recharged with sleep and rest! Meanwhile, Dave could be as exhausted as I was, but he always seemed interested in loving. The fact is, gender differences are often

Your Hormones Affect Your Love Life

The hormonal changes we women go through during pregnancy, nursing, and even our monthly cycles can greatly alter our desire for sex. Although it may seem obvious to us that sex is out of the question on any given night (due to physiological stress or fatigue), we must not assume that our husbands are picking up our signals. My advice is to communicate to your spouse that your lack of interest in sex is based more on physiological issues than a lack of desire or love for him. Find a good reference book, and share a chapter with him addressing the changes in sexual desire that take place as a result of hormonal changes. Assure him that your love life will be reenergized when your hormones level out again.

—Claudia

the most pronounced at this stage of family life. Mothers especially run low on energy.

No matter how tired you are, don't give up on your love life. Do be flexible and responsive. Do talk about your expectations and be realistic. This is a great time to make a list of ways to romance your mate in just a few minutes. For example, in ten minutes or less you can:

- Leave a romantic message on your partner's voice mail.

- Place a flower or love note under his or her windshield wiper.

- Send a card thanking your spouse for being your lover, friend, soul mate.

- Give your partner a foot massage.

- Put a note on the TV saying, "Forget the television. You've already turned me on!"

- Have a "quickie."

Middle Parenting Years: Renewing Expectations for Our Love Life

The first morning that all of our children were finally old enough to go off to school—now that was a great day for us! We were excited to get relief from twenty-four-hour-a-day parenting, more flexibility in our schedule, and more opportunities to revitalize a love life that was stuck in survival mode.

But change isn't easy, and transition times can be risky. Initially, we had different expectations and ideas about how to reinvent our love life. For one thing, our body clocks were different. As we experimented, we discovered that lovemaking was not just reserved for nighttime. With some creative scheduling, we managed to carve out time each week to meet at home without the kids around. That weekly rendezvous was a sex lifesaver for us. We highly recommend it!

"But I just couldn't have sex during the day," one woman confided during a break in one of our seminars. "It just wouldn't seem right."

"Why not?" I asked.

"Well, I'm not sure I could gear down enough in the middle of the day," she responded. "I always have a list of twenty things that need to be done. I just don't think I could get in the mood."

"I remember feeling the same way," I told her. "But I found that my list always waited for me. If I just took the first step, I was always amazed at how much my attitude could change. You should at least give it a try."

As it turned out, her husband agreed with me. And as they talked about their expectations, they designed their own game plan. You can too. Your schedule may not be as flexible as ours, but perhaps you can arrange to leave a few hours late for work or take a long lunch on occasion. Surely, if you and your spouse put your heads together, you can find realistic, creative ways to spend intimate time together while the children are busy at school.

Another thing we recommend during this season is finding friends who are willing to take your children for an evening in return for the same favor. At this stage, you can even plan to leave your children overnight with a trusted friend or sitter from time to time. How often would you like to get away? For how long? Twenty-four hours? A full weekend? A week? Talk, brainstorm, compromise. Agree on what is realistic for you and your kids.

One wife shared a creative idea that works well for her family. "Each month we plan a getaway at a local hotel," she told us. "Since we visit each month, the management willingly gives us a 9 a.m. check-in time. We spend the day as a family, splashing in the swimming pool and using the weightroom. Sometimes we watch a movie. Our kids love it and leave happily when the sitter picks them up in the late afternoon. Then my husband and I have the rest of the evening and the next morning alone, without the kids. It's something we look forward to each month!"

When we heard this, we had to smile. Our kids probably would have left complaining—but they would have left!

Adolescent Parenting Years: Holding on to Our Love Life

For us, major stress reappeared when our kids hit the adolescent years. Talk about misunderstood expectations—and they weren't all concerning our love life! In marriage, few times are more stressful than when you have teenagers in the house.

One, they seem to stay up later than you do, leaving you with very little privacy. Two, they're always having a crisis. It's easy to get so overwhelmed with their problems that you ignore your own.

Talking about our wants, desires, and expectations was critical during those years. We realized that to hang on to our love life, we had to focus on each other and not let our teenagers zap all of our emotional energy. We found four things particularly helpful:

- We claimed Saturday mornings as "our time." Because our teenagers happily slept until noon, we knew we could have some privacy during those hours. Any talk about adolescent issues on Saturday mornings was forbidden.

- We kept our eyes open for opportunities to get away overnight—for example, whenever the kids would go off on a school trip.

- We made the most of those times when everyone was out of the house at football games or other school functions.

- We kept reminding ourselves that "This too shall pass."

The reality is, our kids did finally grow up and leave home. Your kids will also grow up. In the meantime, hang on, keep talking about your expectations, take advantage of whatever "alone time" you have, and plan as many getaways as you can. Let your motto for the adolescent parenting years be "When the kids are away, the parents will play!"

Finally, keep your sense of humor. We have often observed a subtle change in our friends when their kids reach the teenage years. They become more serious and joke less with us. Remember: "This too shall pass!"

Empty Nest Years: Reviving Our Love Life

If you hang in there through the active parenting years, you can eventually reap the benefits of the empty nest. Unfortunately, too many couples reach this marriage milestone with no love life intact. It doesn't have to be that way! Remember the hilarious movie *Father of the Bride II?* The newly pregnant daughter and son-in-law were appalled that her parents were also having a baby—because that meant they still had sex!

When the kids leave the nest, get ready for fun. The whole house is yours again. You have all the privacy you can handle. At this stage you should be more comfortable with one another and be able to enjoy each other more than ever. Don't forget. You still have to make sex a priority; otherwise, other things will crowd it out. We are still workaholics, for example. Even now, if we're not careful, we can get so focused on helping other couples have a great love life that we neglect our own.

Whatever season of life you're in, keep talking about your expectations. Be specific. Be realistic. Seek to meet each other's needs. If you do these things, you can become lifelong lovers, enjoying a creative, satisfying love life at every age.

You can get on the same page—and what a great love story it will be!

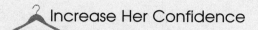

Increase Her Confidence

Letting your wife know how attractive and cherished she is to you is especially important as your children grow up. When children start leaving the nest, many couples struggle, and many relationships end. Don't let the seed of insecurity get planted in your wife's mind at this stage. Continually reassure her of your love and desire for her. Affirm your commitment to her, and you will increase her confidence and her desire for you in return.

—Dave

chapter

6

the time-challenged marriage

"My husband is in graduate school, both of us work full time, and now we're parents. Setting aside time to be together is difficult. We have a two-and-a-half-year-old. I'm away from home eleven hours a day, so when I get home I feel the need to spend time with our son. After feeding and bathing him, I'm exhausted. I can't enjoy time with my husband knowing I'm taking time away from my son, so the time I spend with my husband is usually after our son is in bed, which is late. It's hard on our sex life."

"We're on staff at our church, and often we both have to work evenings. Many nights it's after midnight before we get to bed, and I'm too exhausted to have sex. But my husband—well, he's another story. He seems to always be ready for sex. Last night I looked at him and said, 'What are you doing for lunch tomorrow?' He knew I was too tired, but at least we had a plan for the next day."

"We consider ourselves pretty lucky; my wife has taken a break from her career to stay home with our kids during their preschool years. But we still never seem to have any time together. I have a pretty demanding career, and we thought she would be able to manage the household responsibilities, finances, and church and social obligations while still giving our kids the time they need. Boy, were we wrong. After my thirteen-hour days, I can barely see straight, let alone help out at the house. And after spending the day with our four- and two-year-old kids with no breaks, my wife is a physically and emotionally exhausted wreck. We usually just pop on the TV and fall asleep on the sofa. So much for working on our love life."

"We both travel in our jobs, so we have to work extra hard to find time to connect. Sometimes we don't even know what state the other person is in. Last week we bumped into each other at the Atlanta airport. Neither of us knew the other was in Georgia! Thank goodness for cell phones, but we're not into phone sex. Weekends are so hectic that it's often our love life that gets shortchanged."

Pretty typical comments, wouldn't you say? These survey respondents give voice to the most common complaint we hear from couples about their love lives: "We just don't have time!"

Most marriages are time-challenged in one way or another. All of us have difficulty balancing responsibilities, overcoming time constraints, and battling fatigue. Whatever stage of life we're in, the "sex zapper" of being too rushed is always at our heels. There's just too much to do and too little time to do it!

Let us give you this warning: It's dangerous to get so busy that you neglect your sex life. Once your love life shuts down, it's hard to restart it. Even if you think you can "get by" for now with a sex life that is mediocre or worse, we guarantee you'll arrive at a day in the future when you'll wish you had done more to nurture your love relationship with your spouse.

If you're in your twenties or thirties, you need to know that our research—and personal experience—proves that a sexual relationship can be more satisfying in your forties and beyond than in your early years of marriage. According to a 1994 University of Chicago study, women in their twenties are least likely to achieve orgasm during intercourse. Women in their early forties are most likely! (One reason is that a man's response time slows down as he ages, while a woman's response time speeds up.)[1] Don't ignore or downplay the importance of your love life. Nurture it for today and for the future. *Make* the time. You'll be glad you did.

How Much Time Do You Need?

How much time do you need for a love life? Well, considering that you need time not only for making love but also for building intimacy, our answer is, "As much time as you can make— not find!" *Finding* time is circumstantial; *making* time is intentional. To make time you must aggressively pursue it. You have to be motivated. Here are some practical suggestions:

Make a Commitment

Making time for sex has more to do with your attitude than your circumstances. We make time for those things that are the most important to us. What are your priorities? If you're not sure, think about what you do with your discretionary time and money. Parents: how long has it been since you hired a baby-sitter just so you could have uninterrupted time with one another?

Analyze Your Time Constraints

Keep a record of your activities for one week. What are the nondiscretionary things you do, and how much time do you spend on them? The hours you spend on the job or at the office are probably not very flexible, for instance. What are the things that must be done but have a more flexible time frame? Household responsibilities, family activities, meal preparation, and so on, might fall into this category. Finally, what are the discretionary things you do? For example, how much time do you spend each week on the Internet, watching television and DVDs, reading the paper, golfing, exercising, or playing tennis? How much time do you spend with family and friends?

Now let us meddle a bit. How much time do you spend each week with your mate? Thinking about your mate? Making love? How often do you have dates? How much time do you spend talking with your partner?

What are your main time zappers? What about television and DVDs? In *Super Marital Sex*, Dr. Pearsall writes that "TV addiction is one of the most detrimental influences on American marriage. It is a shared addiction, which is the worst type, because it sometimes covertly robs the relationship of available time for intimacy, while both partners take unknowing part in the theft."[2]

Once you've analyzed the data you've collected, you will probably be able to identify blocks of time that you can reclaim for your love life. Now, go build one with them!

Set Apart Specific Times

Plan specific times that you can dedicate to loving your partner. They can be short or long. For example:

- *Ten-second hugs and kisses.* Each day when you leave and again when you come home, claim ten seconds to hug and kiss. Never mind if you are running late. Ten more seconds will not matter as much as your love life does!

- *Ten minutes to share.* Our mentors, David and Vera Mace, taught us to have a ten-minute sharing time each day—ten minutes when we don't try to solve problems or have sex but just touch emotionally. This has been an invaluable lesson, and we strongly recommend it to you.

- *Weekly date nights.* A regular date night will add immensely to your love life. This standing date is not necessarily for sex. You don't even have to go out. Just carve out some time when you can be alone as a couple without interruptions. (For dating suggestions, see our books *10 Great Dates to Energize Your Marriage* and *52 Fantastic Dates for You and Your Mate.*)[3]

- *Twenty-four-hour getaways.* We've already told you how regular getaways over the years have helped us keep our love life energized. During the parenting years especially, those brief rendezvous enabled us to enjoy a spontaneity that was impossible at home with three boys underfoot. (Parents, pulling off a getaway can be extremely difficult, but don't let the kids stop you. In chapter 13 we'll give you tips for making getaways happen.)

- Candlelit dinners for two. Twice a month, plan a romantic dinner at home. If you have kids, put them to bed early or let them read or watch a favorite DVD while you and your spouse enjoy the intimacy of a beautifully set table and sumptuous, leisurely meal.

Time for Intrigue

Drive in separate cars and meet at a nice restaurant. Pretend you haven't seen each other for several weeks. Invite your spouse to meet you at a hotel. Give him or her the room number and time to arrive. Get there early, and use your imagination to surprise your mate when he or she opens the door

—Dave & Claudia

Use Your Time Twice

Think of ways you can incorporate loving into your daily routine. For example:

- Start a ritual of always making up the bed together each morning and sharing loving thoughts to carry each other through the day.

- Daydream about making love while doing the laundry, the dishes, or other tasks that don't require your full attention.

- Call your mate on your cell phone and talk about your love life while you are doing a mundane chore like folding clothes or filing papers.

- Have the local florist's number preset on your cellular phone and regularly order a special surprise for your spouse.

- Send your spouse an electronic love note while checking your e-mail.

- Light a scented candle and play some romantic music on the CD player or radio while getting ready for bed.

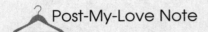 ## Post-My-Love Note

Post-it notes are a favorite of mine. Readily available and portable, they are always handy for emergencies or special surprises. Once when Claudia had hurt her back and was at physical therapy, I left the following note on her car: "Would the lovely, thin, and trim owner of this car hurry to 8624 Dovefield Drive to meet your lover for a romantic rendezvous?"

—Dave

Guard Your Time

If you don't guard your time with each other, no one else will. When you are tempted to make a new time commitment, first ask yourself, "Will what I'm about to commit to bring me closer to my spouse or put distance in our relationship? If I add this to my schedule, what am I willing to drop to balance it?" One of the most helpful things we ever learned how to do was to say *no*—to others, not each other!

Problem-Solving Tips

"But you just don't understand my situation!"

We've heard this comment so many times in our Marriage Alive seminars that we've come up with the following list of ways that couples can make time when there seemingly is none. These ideas do require sacrifice, but the rewards are worth it:

Use Vacation Time

Use annual leave or vacation time to spend uninterrupted hours at home with your spouse. You don't have to take off a whole week, maybe just a day or half a day. Rearrange your schedule to include a couple of hours at home alone without the kids from time to time.

Reduce Your Work Hours

Ask yourself, "Why am I working so hard?" Maybe you don't need more money for more things as much as you need more time for more love. Personally, we would rather spend half as much money on each other and have twice as much time with each other!

Get a New Job

This is an extreme measure and not for everyone. But in some situations, it's the smart thing to do. Years ago Dave was working for a prominent Fortune 500 company that required him to take frequent business trips. I realized that his travel and work schedules were taking a toll on our relationship, but I didn't complain. I figured he was doing what all young, "go-getting" junior executives did. Dave, however, decided that he'd had enough. He loved spending time with his family and didn't think all his extra effort for the company was giving him much in return. He asked to be moved into a position that required less travel, but the company refused. Dave quit on the spot.

I could have strangled him! My shortsighted focus was on the next paycheck—or lack thereof. But Dave had enough confidence in himself and his decision for both of us. Before long, he moved into a position that was much better suited to his temperament and gifts, not to mention more marriage- and family-friendly.

I can look back now and see that quitting the Fortune 500 job was one of the best decisions Dave ever made. While we can't recommend impetuously quitting a job (such an extreme move is rarely practical), we *can* say that making the decision to leave an ill-fitting career and boldly choosing family over that career was the right move for us. It's all too easy to lose sight of what is truly important in life: your spouse, your family, your friends. Why would you intentionally sacrifice truly significant relationships in order to please an impersonal corporation or employer?

Take Care of Your Health

Squeeze in naps, time-outs, and walks around the block. Failing to protect your own health can become a liability to your love life.

Trade Baby-sitting

Parents: Find another family with children and offer to trade baby-sitting duties with them. If you feel you don't know anyone well enough to make this offer, make getting to know some other families a priority. You'd be surprised how many couples are in your same situation and would be thrilled at the suggestion. Introduce yourself to other parents at playgrounds, playgroups, church nurseries, and preschools. Some communities even have baby-sitting co-ops. Approved members trade baby-sitting services, not money, with other members.

Here's a variation on this theme that a survey participant shared with us: "When things get really crazy at our house, I call my best friend who also has preschoolers. I say 'Red Alert!' which lets her know I'm really desperate and need help. If she says it's a 'go,' I call my husband and tell him what time I'm coming to pick him up at the office. Then I make a huge pot of spaghetti, a green salad, and butter two loaves of French bread. I set my table with paper plates for my friend's family and our kids. Next I pack the picnic basket, including a red-checked tablecloth, candles, and a few romantic CDs, with enough spaghetti, salad, and bread for two.

"As soon as my friend—my very good friend—arrives, I leave my kids at home with her and her children, hop in the car, drive to my husband's office, and pick him up. Then we head for a romantic Italian rendezvous at my very good friend's now-empty house. Of course, the next time *I'm* the very good friend!"

Use Those DVDs

We love conducting informal surveys at the many conventions we attend. We get to talk to so many people from so many places around the country in a short period of time. Recently, our standard question has been "How do you find time for sex?" Many answers are amusing, such as this one: "We lock ourselves in the bathroom and tell our kids we have to fix the toilet." But one of the most practical answers came from our friend Greg, the father of two preschoolers.

"That's easy," he said. "As soon as I hear the theme music from *The Lion King,* I become amorous. You don't think we buy all those Walt Disney DVDs and videos for the *kids*, do you? They're for us!"

Don't feel guilty about plopping your kids in front of the TV every now and then. The benefit they will get from two refreshed and reconnected parents will far outweigh any negative impact derived from staring at a television screen for an hour or two.

Creativity Is Still Alive!

We applaud all the couples we've met over the years who are courageously making time for sex. Creativity, we are happy to report, is alive and well! Here's what one survey participant told us:

"When we have time, we love to be creative. We're both very willing to try different things to make it interesting, and we're also not afraid to tell each other if something doesn't feel comfortable or good. Because of the lack of opportunity and time, we've been known to wake up in the middle of the night to have private time. That's desperate, I know, but in some ways it makes us feel a little adventurous, like in the old days!"

This husband and wife have learned how to make time to stay in touch with one another and keep their love life going. They're willing to be creative. They're willing to sacrifice. They're willing to pursue the truly important things.

Now it's your turn. Are you willing to make time for your marriage? Time for intimacy? Time for sex? Make your answer a resounding, enthusiastic Yes! We promise you won't regret it.

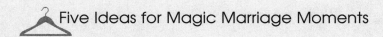 Five Ideas for Magic Marriage Moments

1. Take a shower together and wash each other's hair.

2. Light a candle or oil lantern together and cuddle in the semidarkness.

3. Eat a banana split with two spoons.

4. Give each other a relaxing massage.

5. Order two café au laits and look deeply into each other's eyes.

—Dave & Claudia

chapter

7

the energy-challenged marriage

"I never thought I would ever lack energy for sex," one very tired husband told us. "But after the second baby arrived, I entered a new realm of exhaustion. And now with a toddler and preschooler, things haven't gotten any better. Even on those rare occasions when my wife and I are both awake and interested, we never really relax—especially after what happened last week.

"Here's the scenario: Lately, our love life has been on 'sleep mode.' But last Friday we had plans. Throughout the day we flirted with each other on the phone, at dinner, and as we got the kids in bed. Then, at last, it was our time. We were totally caught up in the romance of the moment, when a little voice standing at the side of our bed said, 'Daddy, can I ride next?' My wife was horrified, and said she would not have sex again until the kids grew up and left home! Any advice?"

Stifling laughter, we responded, "Your heroic efforts to love each other and use energy wisely were really thwarted that time, weren't they? But waiting until the kids grow up is not the answer. A simpler solution is to get a lock on your bedroom door—and use it!"

Obviously, husbands and wives who want to be lovers have a lot of factors to deal with: busy schedules, lack of privacy, and lack of energy, especially during the parenting years. As one survey participant wrote: "Finding the time is easy—just go to bed. Finding the energy is the hard part!"

What can you do when you are just too tired to build a love life? We have three suggestions. First, identify the "energy busters" that are robbing you of your enthusiasm for and interest in sex. Second, consider "energy boosters" that will make you feel better in general and improve your outlook on life. Third, find "energy savers" that will help you have zest left over in your day for romance, intimacy, and sex.

Energy Busters

What are the energy busters in your life—those things that deplete you of physical or emotional strength and compromise your effectiveness as a partner? During the active parenting years, children are at the top of most lists. The truth is, we'd all have more than enough to keep us busy if we did nothing but parent our children. Add careers, home mainte-nance, friends, and community and religious activities, and that's enough to keep anyone busy for several lifetimes. No wonder so many partners complain of having no energy for sex! Here are just a few of the most common energy busters:

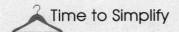

Time to Simplify

No matter how hard we try to compartmentalize our lives, a positive event or habit in one area of life posi-tively affects all other areas of life, just as a negative event or habit can detrimentally impact other seem-ingly unrelated areas. Our advice? Streamline and sim-plify your life so your energies are going only to those things that positively impact your love life and family.

—Dave & Claudia

Too Many Commitments

If you're like most couples, you have too much to do. Of course, some of your pressing commitments are long-term, and they're worthy efforts. Frankly, you might be hard pressed to get out of them. But having too many outside commitments can be detrimental to your marriage and your love life.

Take a hard look at how you spend your time and figure out which activities you can easily eliminate from your schedule (usually the ones that don't affect anyone else).

Then think about which additional activities you may also need to let go. As hard as it is to disappoint a friend, relative, or coworker, you need to say *no* to those energy zappers that take up too much of your personal time, your time with your family, and your time and energy for love.

To help make the hard choices, ask yourself three questions:

- *Is this activity essential?* Would the sky fall in if I don't do this? Essential activities would include such things as earning a living, caring for your children, sleeping, and eating.

- *Is this activity really important?* Will it help me to be a better spouse or parent? Personally, we've decided that a healthy diet, exercise, devotions, prayer, and regular dates with each other enhance our relationship and therefore are really important.

- *Is this activity discretionary?* Is it optional—my choice— something I would simply *like* to do? Discretionary activities might include civic and community activities or more personal things like watching television, staying after work on Friday evenings for social hour, shopping, or golfing.

Deciding which discretionary activities to drop is tough. Often these pursuits seem important and even beneficial to your family. For instance, volunteering at a homeless shelter may indeed benefit your family because it gives you an opportunity to model appropriate citizen behavior for your children. But if your volunteering is done at the expense of your marriage relationship, then it's detrimental and needs to go. (One way around this is to volunteer as a couple and spend that time together.)

No Time for Me

"I invest my time and energy meeting everyone else's needs," one survey participant wrote. "There's no time left over for just me. I feel as if I'm losing myself."

Everyone needs personal time. The lack of any real time to yourself is a big energy buster. What are those things that help you regroup emotionally and restore your energy reserves? Some activities may seem frivolous compared to your more "serious" responsibilities, but times of personal refreshment and renewal need to be built into your schedule and guarded as fiercely as any other important activities—for your sake and the sake of your love life.

No Exercise and Poor Diet

Nothing zaps energy as much as a high-fat, high-sugar diet with little or no exercise. So much has been written and reported about the way diet and exercise affect energy levels that we have no excuse for not making the necessary changes in our lifestyles. We'll look at this area in greater depth when we discuss specific ways to increase energy.

Unequal Division of Labor

Are you tired all the time, while your partner always manages to get a full night's sleep and plenty of recreation and relaxation? Surprisingly, this is a common scenario in marriages. We're all familiar with the stereotype: the wife who assumes that she must single-handedly do the dishes and the laundry, help with the kids' homework, give baths, clean the bathrooms, and pick up the house—all while her husband is watching the news or falling asleep in the recliner after his long day at work. Hogwash! Both partners should share the household load. If both partners are putting forth equal effort throughout the day, whether at work or at home, and if the husband finishes up at six o'clock while his wife still has three hours to go, then the husband should offer to chip in—or vice versa. Sharing responsibility and working together ensures that neither you nor your partner has to carry too heavy a burden and that no misplaced resentment develops between you.

No Structure

Another energy buster is lack of structure. Some couples need more structure in their lives than others, but everyone needs some! Otherwise, instead of proactively balancing responsibilities, you end up simply responding to crises and "putting out fires"—a sure recipe for zapping energy and putting out the one fire you want to keep burning: your love life.

Both of us are spontaneous people. We like surprises and

flexibility. But our love life would never have survived all these years if we had not imposed some structure on our schedules. For example, when our boys were young, we had a general routine: naps or quiet times after lunch, dinner around 6:30 p.m., and bedtime rituals that included bathtime, stories, prayers, and cuddles. Our schedule wasn't rigid, and some days we completely scrapped it. But having a basic plan for each day helped us to pace ourselves and allowed us to have energy (at least sometimes) for each other after the children were snug in their beds.

Energy Boosters

When you're tired and lacking stamina, it's hard to imagine having a fun, energized love life. By taking just a few simple steps, you can increase your energy level and have enough energy not only to take care of your responsibilities but also to love your spouse. You don't have to wait to find energy for sex. Here are some ways you can boost your energy right now:

Take Care of Yourself

You must be good to yourself before you can be good to others. You must nurture your own mind, body, and spirit before you can take care of the needs of the other people in your life. Resist feeling guilty about the time you take away from other things to take care of yourself. You aren't being selfish; you're modeling healthy living. Consider these four common-sense tips for taking care of yourself:

Stay Intellectually Stimulated

If you are a stay-at-home parent, work at keeping your mind active. Stay in touch with the world outside. You'll be a better parent, a better conversationalist with your spouse, and be more likely to have higher self-esteem. As one survey participant wrote, "I realized I needed to find ways to stay intellectually stimulated when I talked to a telemarketing person for fifteen minutes one day. I just wanted to talk to another adult!"

What are some ways to stay intellectually stimulated?

- Listen to news and interviews on talk radio.
- Read a weekly news magazine.
- Keep a journal.
- Call one adult friend each day.
- Attend a monthly lecture.
- Join a monthly book club or a safe Internet chat line on an interesting subject.
- Learn French, German, Spanish, or the foreign language of your choice.

Get Regular Exercise

Thirty minutes of aerobic exercise three times each week is the minimum recommendation of most health professionals for maintaining physical health. You don't have to join a health club or buy expensive exercise equipment. Simply taking a brisk walk three or four times a week can make a big difference in how you feel. Even five minutes of daily stretching can raise your physical fitness level, which will increase your energy for loving your partner.

Check with your doctor, then begin to make exercise a habit—a set part of your weekly schedule. Think you don't have time to stay in shape? Try some of these suggestions:

- Do push-ups using the kitchen counter.
- Jump rope.
- Walk and talk with a friend while pushing the stroller.
- Lie on your back and lift your baby instead of weights.
- Walk up and down the stairs for ten minutes.
- When you go shopping, park a couple of blocks away from the store.

Watch Your Diet

Eating well is a sure way to boost your energy level. Cutting out high-fat foods will make you feel less sluggish, while adding high-energy foods such as whole-grain pasta, nuts, and yogurt will support you throughout the day. Choose healthy snacks such as apples, oranges, bananas, raisins, or raw vegetables with non- or low-fat dip. Try to drink eight glasses of water each day, perhaps with a slice of lemon or lime for flavor.

To get a better handle on ways to maximize your energy through healthy eating, read a good, balanced book on nutrition. You may also want to consider adding high-energy vitamins to your daily diet. Check with your doctor first before you make any drastic changes in your eating habits or start taking any strange-sounding supplements that make fantastic-sounding promises.

Nurture Yourself

As we've said, everyone needs personal time. Make an effort to carve out some personal time to nurture yourself—daily if possible. This may mean taking fifteen minutes after the kids go to bed to sit quietly in a darkened room to de-stress. It may mean slipping off alone for a quiet cup of coffee during your break at work. Grab personal time wherever you can find it. You won't be the only one who benefits!

When our boys were young, one important thing I did for myself was to establish a daily time for devotions and reflection. In a notebook I journaled my thoughts and concerns and recorded specific prayers. This personal time helped me to connect with my heavenly Father and renew my spirit. I was able to put life in perspective, and I was a much nicer mom and mate as a result! Of course, I had to be flexible to find this time. It didn't happen every single day; but because I intentionally sought it, I found it more days than not.

Restructure Your Life

The second step toward boosting your energy level is to restructure your life. Sounds like a big task, doesn't it? It doesn't have to be. The key is to be honest about your needs and priorities and then be creative in how you approach your particular time constraints. If you really have to stay late at work three nights each week, for example, consider going in late to work one day a week so you can spend a leisurely breakfast with your partner. If you're a stay-at-home mom and you regularly find yourself exhausted by the time the weekend arrives, hire a neighborhood teenager to play with your kids for a couple of hours every Friday afternoon so you can take a nap or regroup.

Consider four areas of your life that may need a little restructuring:

Household Chores

If you have children, recruit them—even if they're small. You may be surprised at how much toddlers enjoy helping! A two-year-old we know loves to help his mommy mop the floor. She sprays wood soap in a small area, and he scrubs his little heart out in all of the bubbles. Choose age-appropriate tasks, and remember that teaching your children to pitch in is not only helpful to you but also it's an important part of their learning process. How else will they know how to do such things when they grow up and have homes of their own? (For a guide to know what your children are capable of doing and not doing, we recommend the excellent book *Children Who Do Too Little* by Patricia Sprinkle.)[1]

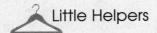 ## Little Helpers

Young children can be helpers—especially if you lower your standards! Here are some suggestions for age-appropriate help:

Ages Two to Four

- Pick up toys
- Clean up dropped food
- Help Mommy dust—especially the floor
- Make simple decisions, such as choosing between two foods
- Do simple hygiene (brush teeth, wash and dry hands)

Ages Four to Six

- Set the table
- Put groceries away
- Feed pets
- Dust furniture
- Make the bed

Elementary School

- Choose clothes for the day
- Be a kitchen helper
- Make a simple school lunch
- Water the plants
- Clean the bedroom
- Take phone messages
- Begin to learn how to use the washer and dryer

—Jean Lush with Pamela Vredevelt[2]

Naps and Bedtime

Make your kids' naptimes and bedtimes count for your good. Instead of collapsing on the couch in front of the television, do something that is truly relaxing and nurturing, such as taking a bath, having a cup of tea, or reading a good book. Or make the time superproductive: Blitz it. You'll be amazed at how much you can accomplish in just one hour without the constant interruptions of small children. On those days when you're just plain exhausted, take a nap yourself!

Obligations

To boost your energy level, you really need to keep your outside commitments to a minimum. Not an easy task, we know. There's so much to do, and so many people wanting your time and attention. To help you, we've come up with the following list of five ways to say no:

1. "I've done it in the past, and I'll do it again in the future; but I can't do it at present."
2. "I'm sorry. I'll just have to pass this time."
3. "I'm flattered you asked, but I'll have to say no this time."
4. "No."
5. Here's a five-star no to use in emergencies: "No! I have no desire, time, or energy. It's simply impossible! No!"

Energy Savers

Let's say you and your spouse have identified your energy busters. You've added several key energy boosters to your daily lives. Still, it's hard for the two of you to get everything done that needs to be done and still have some energy left over for a love life. You need more than energy boosters; you need energy savers!

Some energy savers may seem like "small potatoes," but they can add up to big surpluses of energy for loving—things like not answering the phone after 9 p.m., showering together, reading books together, and taking a "divide and conquer" approach to evening chores. Then there's the big gun: enlisting help from others. Look for friends, family members, or others who can give you a break, help you accomplish certain tasks, or simply provide a listening ear when you're at the end of your rope. Help is out there—you just have to find it.

Here are some creative ways our survey participants have found to enlist help:

- "I get together with some other moms, and we share chores such as going to the grocery store. One of us watches all the children while the others shop."

- "When it gets crazy, I fax my grocery list to a full-service store and pick up my groceries later or have them delivered."

- "I can't afford a weekly housekeeper, but I have

someone come in and give my house a good, deep cleaning twice a month."

- "I use a twelve-year-old neighborhood girl as my 'mother's helper.' She entertains my preschoolers while I clean the house or take a nap. She may not be the most reliable sitter in the world—I don't leave her completely alone with the children—but she is affordable, and she has endless energy to throw the ball or paint or color.

Weekend Perk-Me-Ups

- On Saturday afternoons we tell the kids that we need a nap, and we are not to be disturbed unless the house is on fire. We always invite them to take a nap too. They are horrified at the thought and disappear.

- Often we awaken before the alarm goes off . . . that's the time when we are physically fresh.

- Sundays after church we come home, put on a special DVD for the kids, and tell them not to disturb us because we'll be very busy "cleaning our room."

- Sometimes we get a baby-sitter just for a couple of hours and stay home together instead of going out.

- Saturday morning cartoons are awesome!

—Survey Participants

Plus, in the future she will be a great sitter—already trained and familiar to my kids!"

- "I joined a co-op playgroup. This gives me two or three hours of free time each week."

- "When our last baby was born, we hired a personal chef for the first few weeks."

Energy for Loving

Energy, like time, is one of the most precious commodities your love life will ever have. Cherish the energized moments you have with your spouse, and make the most of every day. Don't forget to put the tips from this chapter into practice. Even if your marriage is energy-starved, you can build a strong, creative love life together—and maybe have a little energy to spare.

8

putting marriage first:
tips for parents

"I don't know how it came to this!" Ellen sobbed. "Where did we go wrong?"

Marshall, Ellen's husband of eighteen years, had just packed his bags and moved out.

"In the beginning of our marriage, we had such a good relationship," Ellen told us. "Our sex life was great. As a matter of fact, life for the two of us was so good that we weren't sure we wanted to have kids. But after a number of years, my biological clock started running out of time, and we made that big decision to start a family. Within a year Hailey was born, and two years later, Nathan came along.

"Frankly, we didn't know what hit us! With our first baby, we were both nervous and overprotective. Hailey was high-strung, which didn't help at all. I began bringing her into bed with me and nursing her to sleep. Sometimes I was so tired, I didn't have the energy to get up and put her back in her crib. It's not easy having children in your late thirties. Marshall wouldn't want to wake us, so he would sleep in the guest room or on the couch. Unfortunately, this became a pattern—one that continued when Nathan was born.

"Now our children are six and eight. In addition to all their daytime demands, they still expect me to lie down with them when they go to bed. I'm basically a morning person, and after the hassle of getting them settled at night, there's nothing left of me to give to Marshall. Our intimate times together over the last several years have been sketchy. I should have seen it coming. It's been weeks—no, to be honest, it's been months—since we've had sex."

Ellen acknowledged that her parenting role had overshadowed her role as a spouse. "I've felt more like a mom than a sexy wife," she admitted.

Did Ellen make mistakes? Yes, but Marshall wasn't off the hook. Apparently, he'd taken a passive role in maintaining their marriage and their love life. He'd chosen to focus most of his time and energy on building his company and getting ahead. "You do that," he later told us, "by working hard and working long hours. With Ellen so committed to the children, there wasn't much to come home for anyway. Finally, I realized we didn't even know each other anymore. We didn't have a personal relationship, much less a sexual one. I thought it was time to get on with my life. I'm not getting any younger, you know."

What's wrong with this picture? How could a couple who had a great relationship and love life the first ten years of their marriage lose it after the children came along? What could they have done differently? What message were they passing on to their kids about the sanctity of marriage by splitting up?

Is it possible to be good parents and build a good marriage at the same time? Our emphatic answer is Yes! But you must put your marriage—not your kids—first. Putting kids first not only damages your marriage but also sets the wrong example for your children and destabilizes their home environment. Our advice: love your children dearly, but teach them to respect your marriage and your need for time alone together. That way they'll grow up to be healthy, secure adults who are others-centered and who recognize the importance of the marriage relationship.

One of the best things you and your spouse can do for your kids is to love each other. Children feel more secure when they know their parents' marriage relationship is strong, loving, and healthy. Our boys would roll their eyes and say, "Mom and Dad are at it again!" whenever they would catch us hugging and kissing—which was quite often. That was life at the Arps' house! We were determined to be affectionate with each other and to protect our "just-for-two" times. We never felt guilty when we locked our bedroom door.

Over the years, through the school of experience, we learned several key ways to teach our children to respect our relationship and our need for time alone:

- We created our own private space.
- We cultivated our own private times.
- We let our children see us being affectionate and let them ask questions about our marriage relationship.
- We built friendships with other couples.
- We practiced the "Four Rs."

Let's take a closer look at each of these five keys.

Private Space

A great sex life is dependent upon having a place to be intimate. With no privacy, there can be little romance. One wife told us, "Our house is great for our kids, the pets, our friends, company—but it doesn't work so well for my husband and me. We have no privacy. Our kids wander in and out of our bedroom like it's Grand Central Station!"

"Then it's time to railroad them out of your bedroom," we responded, "and close the door!"

It's critical that you and your spouse have your own private space in your home. We do mean physical space, whether it's your bedroom, study, or even the master bathroom. It's a space where your children must have special permission to enter. For most couples, the bedroom is the logical choice. Resist making your bedroom do double-duty as a family room, office, or sewing room. Instead, make it a sanctuary where you can be alone as a couple and focus on loving each other—a refuge from the overwhelming needs and general chaos of family life.

Once you've claimed your space, add whatever touches you need to create a loving and romantic atmosphere. Toys are out, and candles are in! If your finances are limited and you have to choose which room in the house to upgrade first, choose your bedroom or master bath. Wherever we've lived, we've always created a sitting area in our bedroom—even when the room has been quite small—so we could have a place to retreat from our kids and read or talk in peace and quiet. When we built our condo home, we treated ourselves to a dream bathroom getaway: dual showerheads; a Jacuzzi tub; a chandelier for candles, not electric lights; and a basket of fresh towels, bath salts, and body oils.

Next, teach your children to knock before entering! We found that our boys could learn to knock at an early age. We also discovered that if we wanted them to respect our private space, we had to respect theirs. We always did what we could to provide each of our sons with his own space, even if it meant being creative with room dividers, curtains, and bookcases. As the boys grew older, we tried to remember to knock before entering and to respect their right to create an environment that was comfortable to them (within certain parameters, of course).

What if your children are small and need almost constant supervision? Invest in one or more nursery monitors (turned down low, but loud enough to hear if a crisis erupts). Then close the bedroom or bathroom door, and rest assured that you'll be alerted if the baby wakes up or the kids get into a fight.

How to Have a Five-Star Bedroom on a One-Star Budget

- Add candles, candles, and more candles (don't forget scented ones).
- Enhance the mood with music. Put a CD or DVD player in your bedroom and invest in a few CDs. Even an inexpensive radio will work; there are a number of great classical and easy-listening stations that can help create a romantic atmosphere.
- Add a dimmer switch to your overhead light.
- Add inexpensive ambience with a grouping of comfortable pillows on the bed.
- Frame and display pictures of the two of you together.
- Buy matching bathrobes.

—Dave & Claudia

Private Times

Setting aside a romantic, private space is a start—but you need to use it! You need to have private times in that private space. We suggest that you establish two types of private times: *adult time,* when your kids are around but you're focusing on your partner, not them; and *alone time,* when your children are safely in bed or otherwise occupied in their own rooms, and you can concentrate on loving.

Adult Time

As soon as your children are old enough to understand, teach them about *adult time.* Start with short blocks of time and explain to them that they must find something besides you to occupy their attention for that period. Even if the time is too short for you and your spouse to escape to your private hideaway, you can at least sit on the sofa and talk and cuddle. The sooner your kids learn to entertain themselves, the easier it will be to increase the number and length of adult times you have together.

Alone Time

Alone time is often harder to find than adult time, but there's one sure way to get it: set and enforce a bedtime for your children. Did we hear you groan? Of course, bedtimes will change as your children grow up; and you can count on occasional disruptions to the routine. But knowing your children will be in their rooms after a certain time allows you to plan special moments and increases your anticipation of the bedtime hour.

If your children already have a bedtime routine, but their bedtime is too late and you're exhausted by the time they're asleep, change your nightly ritual and move everything up thirty to sixty minutes. Your children may not go right to sleep (and count on them complaining!), but at least they can stay in their rooms. Older children can read, listen to tapes, or do other quiet activities. Don't feel guilty. You're fighting for your marriage here! If the only way you can find some private time for loving (and we don't mean half-asleep sex) is to enforce an earlier bedtime, do it. Your marriage will benefit, and ultimately your children will too.

Of course, other demands will zap some of your time after your kids are in bed—the dishes must be done, clothes must be washed, bills must be paid. However, don't let your efforts to set aside time for loving go to waste. Other things can wait. Make your love life your priority.

Open Affection

Your children need to realize that the relationship between you and your spouse is distinct, special, and not dependent upon them. They need to learn that they are *not* the center of your universe—that your marriage existed before they arrived and will continue after they leave. As we've said, they will feel more secure and loved as you model a healthy marriage. They'll also have a good point of reference for their own future romantic relationships.

The level of affection parents are comfortable displaying in front of their children will vary from couple to couple. You don't want to get *too* intimate. But generally speaking, it's healthy for your children to overhear loving remarks and see you holding hands, cuddling on the couch, and kissing. When our boys were growing up, we didn't hide the love notes we left for each other on the kitchen counter or office door; and while we didn't discuss our love life with them, they were aware of why we liked to go away for the weekend or have time alone in our bedroom.

By seeing your open affection, your children learn practical, healthy ways for couples to express love to one another. Remember, you're modeling. Just think how good you'll feel when your kids are grown and married, and you see them leaving notes, sending flowers, and taking special weekends away with their spouses!

Adult Friendships

This may seem like an odd principle to include in a book about improving your love life, but cultivating adult friendships reinforces the notion that there is an adult world and a child's world. While the two worlds often intersect, they are distinct and important in their own right. Through your adult friendships, you provide models of other marriage relationships and broaden your children's frame of reference. Your kids also see that you aren't the only adults in the world who like to hold hands or cuddle (thereby making you more like everyone else and less "creepy" when you show affection).

Invite your adult friends to your home from time to time. The younger your children are when you start this, the better, because they'll accept "having company" as a normal part of their lives. If you find that they fight to be the center of attention whenever company is present, work to change their behavior. Be persistent. Bring out a special toy that they like but don't often get to play with. Give them a new book they are eager to read. Let them watch a special TV program or invite a friend to sleep over. Remind them, "This is adult time." They'll eventually get the hang of it.

"Just-You-and-Me" Times

We found that when we spent private time with each of our children, they were more willing to accept that Mom and Dad needed private time together or with adult friends. At an early age we initiated "Just-You-and-Me" times—times we spent alone with one child to talk, kick the soccer ball, visit the library, or go out for hot chocolate. Our "Just-You-and-Me" times were not always large blocks of time. Sometimes as little as ten or fifteen minutes in the kitchen with cookies and milk were sufficient to get that "just two" feeling.

—Dave & Claudia

The "Four Rs"

The "Four Rs" are four basic, tried-and-true principles that we like to emphasize in all of our parenting seminars. They can apply to all stages in the parenting process. Putting them into practice gives you the confidence to be thoughtful, intentional parents and helps you face almost any parenting dilemma. By following the Four Rs, you can spend less time and energy in a state of parental confusion and stress—and have more time and energy to focus on your love life.

Regroup

Occasionally, you need to regroup and reevaluate the status of your children's development and your parenting approach. Children go through different developmental stages, necessitating changes in the ways you relate to them. Some stages are more difficult than others and require you to work together with your spouse more than others. We encourage you to read a book or two about the stages of child development with your partner and set aside regular times to discuss your children's development, growth, and individual needs.

Relate

The key to raising healthy, happy children is the quality of the parent-child relationship. That's why, instead of overemphasizing minor issues like how your children dress or whether they're involved in enough extracurricular activities, you need to spend time building your relationship with your kids, demonstrating your love and commitment to them. The security they develop from having a close relationship with Mom and Dad will provide them with the internal resources they'll need to face the challenges of life. That's far more important than how well their outfits coordinate or how tidy their rooms are.

Release

Your kids will only be with you for a short time. They will eventually grow up, move away, go to college, get married, and start their own families. That means that for your benefit and theirs, you have to approach parenting from the perspective that it's a temporary job with the goal of developing a mature human being who can live successfully without you. As your children grow, you must encourage them, in age-appropriate ways, to take increasing responsibility for their own decisions and lives. At the same time, you must focus on solidifying the relationships in your own life that will last—especially the one with your spouse.

Relax

Parenting should be a pleasure. Marriage should be a pleasure. Give yourself permission to have fun with your kids and with your mate. Take time to laugh. Be spontaneous. Pace yourself. Periodically take a short break just for you so that you can be refreshed, renewed, and better able to meet the challenges of being a parent and a spouse. (For more tips on how to establish the Four Rs and develop a game plan to get

126

your children through the adolescent years, see our book *Suddenly They're 13—or the Art of Hugging a Cactus.*)[1]

Your children can enrich your marriage. Your marriage can enrich your children. The two can work together so wonderfully—but only if you put your marriage first.

part
3

in just a little while...

you can enjoy lovin' that
just keeps getting better!

chapter
9

love à la carte

"Sex isn't as important as bread and water," one husband commented in our survey, "but it's right up there near the top!"

Bread, water, sex—all three are critical necessities for a healthy love life. And all three have much in common. In fact, people frequently use food analogies when talking about sex. "I'm starved for love," someone might say. "Our sexual appetites are so different," another might complain.

At different stages of life, your appetite and tastes in food vary. Similarly, at different stages of marriage, your sexual appetite varies, as does the fare that you can realistically expect to order off your "love menu." "Gourmet sex," for example, may be a rare treat in a time-starved marriage. You may not get it often, but when you do, it's wonderful! "Fast food," meanwhile, has its place; but if it makes up the sum total of your love diet, your marriage will lack important vitamins, and the health of your relationship will suffer.

Even during high-stress times, you need to have a balanced diet of sex and love. To help you achieve that, we've designed a Love à la Carte menu. Look over the menu and think about what sounds appetizing to you. What would your partner enjoy?

Remember, an à la carte menu is just that—à la carte! You can pick and choose selections that sound appetizing to you and your spouse. Compromise is important. If something sounds too far out to one or both of you, please skip it. We are quite traditional ourselves; and while our love life is alive and well, some of the suggestions we read in other books cause us to look at each other and say, "No way! Don't even think about it!"

As we've emphasized before, identifying and communicating your expectations are essential to having a healthy love life. Our Love à la Carte menu will help you voice your expectations and discuss one another's wants and needs. Sit down with your partner and select a healthy diet of intimacy and sex from the menu that follows. For your convenience, we've divided it into four courses: appetizers, snacks and fast foods, main courses, and desserts.

Appetizers

Appetizers create interest, increase appetite, and precede a main course. They should:

- Be light

- Be easy to prepare

- Please the taste buds

- Whet your appetite for the main course

On a Love à la Carte menu, an appetizer is a come-on, an invitation. It's any word or action that increases your sexual desire and pleasure.

We still remember the night we were sitting at Kelly's Restaurant just south of Myrtle Beach, South Carolina. We had managed to pull the ultimate coup and slip away from our kids for a getaway. Our appetizer started with that certain look across the table and our feet moving under it. We held hands while our feet pursued their own agenda. In the parking lot we stopped and kissed before heading back to our condo. The drive back had its intimate moments, which we won't describe. When we got to the condo, we continued to kiss and cuddle in the car. One thing led to another. We remember that evening for its great sex, preceded by great appetizers!

You don't have to get away from home and kids to share an appetizer. You can whet your partner's appetite with a phone call that says, "I love you and I'm thinking about you." You might slip a love note in your partner's briefcase or bring home a gift of one long-stemmed red rose. A good appetizer might be a backrub, a playful caress, or a shower for two in a candlelit bathroom. It might be a few moments of cuddling on the couch after the kids are in bed, listening to your favorite music, or watching a romantic movie together.

The all-time best appetizer? We vote for kissing. So do Clifford and Joyce Penner, authors of the book *52 Ways to Have Fun, Fantastic Sex.* They write: "Kissing is an indicator of the quality of a sexual relationship. When kissing is pas-

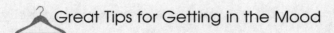 Great Tips for Getting in the Mood

- Flirt with each other. Even when there isn't time for sex, make sure your mate knows you want to. If you communicate your desire for him, it keeps his fire lit.
- Keep up a nice amount of tension, using body language and little whispers, to help keep the mood going until you are free to do something about it. This gets you prepared in mind and body and pushes out unwanted emotions that may try to intrude in the interim.
- Spend time talking together about the day, and if possible, pray together.
- Take a short walk together and hold hands.
- Relax with a cup of tea and turn off the TV.
- Let your mate know that you want to spend time alone with her, that she is the center of the universe for you at this moment.

—Survey Participants

sionate, warm, and deep, and when it's an ongoing part of a couple's relationship, they likely have a satisfying sexual relationship."[1]

Sex must never become so goal-oriented that long, passionate kisses disappear from the repertoire. If kissing goes, so does some of the pleasure and intimacy of being together.

One last point about appetizers: they don't have to lead immediately to the main course. In fact, sometimes it's better if they don't. A good appetizer can help balance differences in sexual desire by tempering sexual cravings for the hungrier partner and increasing desire for the one who isn't so hungry. The eventual result is a wonderful, full-course meal for both!

Snacks and Fast Foods

Snacks and fast foods alleviate hunger for a brief period of time. They're a quick treat, a minimeal. Snacks and fast foods should:

- Be easy to prepare
- Not totally quench the appetite
- Not be the total diet
- Taste (feel) good

When it comes to sex, snacks are similar to appetizers, except they're a little more substantial and usually include the act of making love. In the parenting years (and other periods of high stress), it's easy to get stuck on "fast food" sex. It's quick and easy and doesn't require much in the way of time or energy. Like a trip to McDonald's, "fast food" sex is okay from time to time; but as a steady diet, it's not the healthiest source of long-term marital nutrition.

Still, it has its place, particularly when it comes to bridging the gap between a husband and wife who are experiencing different levels of sexual desire. In the early years of marriage, men have a quicker response time than women, and they tend to have more sexual tension to release. Adding to this discrepancy, men tend to compartmentalize sex; women don't. Generally speaking, women need love and intimacy to give sex, while men need sex to give love and intimacy. All of this adds up to different needs at different times. That's when snacks can help.

One snack we simply call the "quickie." It's when one partner says, "Honey, I'm just not up to a main course tonight; but what about a quickie?" Perhaps you are just too exhausted or have no huge appetite for sex on a particular night. At such a time, giving your spouse a gift of love and willingly meeting his or her needs through a brief encounter can actually build intimacy and closeness. It also relieves you from the feeling that you have to "fake it." Pretending to respond when you aren't responding is deceptive and detrimental to your relationship. In the end, it only destroys intimacy.

Snacks are sometimes more important for one partner than the other. I remember one weekend getaway when our children were really small, and my sexual appetite was really big. When we arrived at the mountain cabin on a Friday night, we were both tired. Claudia, being a morning person, was especially tired, but she gladly agreed to a quickie. This relieved my built-up sexual tension. The rest of the weekend, I was able to concentrate on pleasing her, and together we crafted a weekend menu that was satisfying and pleasing for both of us.

Here are some other snacks to try:

- Ten minutes of nondemand touching
- Only pleasuring one partner
- A midnight or early morning surprise
- Old-fashioned petting

Main Courses

Main courses satisfy hunger, give energy and strength, and provide nutrients and vitamins needed for health and growth. Main courses should:

- Be well-balanced
- Not be consumed too quickly
- Have variety
- Be appetizing to both partners
- Satisfy deep hunger

Main courses in your love life take time and usually require planning. While every time you make love will not and cannot be a "main course," for a healthy love diet, you need planned times. So go ahead, make an appointment! As one survey participant suggests, "When you can't have the privacy you want when you want it, make an appointment with one another and be prepared to stick to it, unless physical illness precludes intimacy." Another wife adds: "It's difficult to find time, but planning helps. Setting a date makes it possible. It gives you time to plan and gives you something to look forward to."

When planning main courses, though, be sure to avoid the "same old, same old." Even your favorite entrée becomes tasteless if that's all you ever eat.

"Don't get stuck in a rut," one survey participant recommends. "Any time of day or night needs to remain an option.

Plan Main Courses

To add main courses to your already busy life, go on and make that love calendar that we mentioned in an earlier chapter. Sit down with your spouse, talk over your schedule, and begin to block out times for main courses. By writing these times and dates on your calendar, you'll be prompted to find sitters, make reservations, and set aside funds.

While you're at it, why not make a list of main courses that sound appetizing to both of you, and assign them to specific dates?

—Dave & Claudia

And get away alone for a night or two frequently."

Another writes: "Your bedroom isn't the only appropriate place for lovemaking. Go to a motel one night, or go camping. Use good judgment, discretion, and imagination—it can lead to a lot of fun."

Desserts

Desserts complete a wonderful meal, satisfy a sweet tooth, and bring little pleasures. Desserts should:

- Be special

- Compliment the main course

- Not always be necessary

Dessert is that little bit of sweetness—that special feeling of closeness and intimacy—that tops off a great main course. It's especially important to a woman. It's important to a man too; he just may not admit it! A dessert doesn't always have to follow a big meal, however. Sometimes it can be enjoyed alone—as just a little "something" to sweeten the relationship.

Here are a few Desserts à la Love to consider. Can you think of other sweeteners to add to the list?

- Verbal expressions of affection

- Ten minutes of after-play

- Two cups of chai tea and love talk

- Snuggling before going to sleep

- Lying on a blanket outdoors and gazing at the stars

Setting the Table

Years ago I made a great discovery: Even if Dave and I were eating leftovers, if I set an attractive table, the meal tasted better. Candlelight could even make peanut butter and jelly sandwiches taste good! The same is true for loving. Whatever items you choose from the Love à la Carte menu, your enjoyment and pleasure will be increased if you make an effort to "set a lovely table." For example, try incorporating:

- Candlelight
- Romantic music
- Perfume
- Incense
- Flowers
- Silk pajamas
- Silk sheets

—Claudia

Plan Your Own Menu

Equipped with a few good ideas, an understanding of one another's needs and desires, and your own imagination, you and your spouse are now ready to create a mutually satisfying menu for loving. So get out your calendar, plan a month's worth of pleasuring, and go to it! Along the way, make sure to note which menu items you both enjoy and which items you'd rather send back to the kitchen. Remember, your tastes will change from time to time. Just keep loving each other and talking to each other, and the rest will follow.

Bon appètit!

chapter 10

scheduling sex

Whenever we write about sex, we get responses. Here are a couple of the letters we got in response to an article titled "Help for a Harried Sex Life":

"Can you help? We're having a problem with intimacy," one reader wrote. "We had a great love life during the first part of our marriage. We were spontaneous, and romance was alive. Then we got involved in building our careers, and our times for loving were fewer and fewer. But since the kids came along—we have three preschoolers ages one, two, and three—we have a real problem with intimacy.

"Frankly, after having three children climb on me all day, I just don't want to be touched. I want my 'personal space' back. I end up making myself be intimate, because I know my husband wants sex. My husband knows I'm doing this, and it doesn't help our love life at all. Sex has become very routine and mechanical. In addition, I've put on forty pounds since my first pregnancy, and my self-image has been affected. On top of it all, I'm exhausted.

"Do you have any suggestions for my seemingly hopeless sexual relationship? How can we get back a little of the spontaneity and romance and reignite a faltering love life?"

While this reader's situation is desperate, we wouldn't classify it as hopeless! In the deep, dark recesses of her mind are memories of a brighter day and an enjoyable love life. But if she is expecting spontaneity and romance to suddenly reappear, she is dreaming. Revitalizing a flat love life is hard work; but step by step, it can be done.

Another reader wrote, "My husband and I just celebrated our fifth wedding anniversary. We have a three-and-a-half-year-old daughter and another child on the way. The scenarios described in your article are foreign to us; we have had no problems maintaining a good marriage and sex life after the arrival of children.

"We put our daughter to bed at 8:00 p.m. each night. My husband and I do not retire until 10:00 p.m. This leaves us two hours of peace, quiet, and togetherness each night. We have taught our daughter right from the beginning that once she is in bed, she stays in bed. She is strong-willed, but we have no trouble maintaining peace at bedtime because this routine is strictly enforced, and she has learned that it does no good to fight it. So my husband and I can look forward to the last two hours of each day. We have time to sit and talk, enjoy our hot tub, watch a movie together, or be romantic."

Harried sex lives aren't just reserved for partners who are parents. Maybe you're trying to balance the two-job tightrope, and you have little time left over for a love life. Or maybe you have some "soft addictions" that eat up time that could be spent on loving—things like spending too much time surfing the Internet, watching television, or shopping.

Whatever your situation, we're convinced your love life will benefit from one recommendation in particular: start scheduling sex. If sex on a schedule doesn't sound romantic to you, think again. Planning sex can help reignite the spark in your love life and lead to future, more spontaneous times.

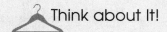 **Think about It!**

Your sexual relationship progresses or regresses in direct proportion to how much attention you give it.

—Dave & Claudia

Reigniting the Spark

In a *Ladies Home Journal* poll, 1,500 readers in their thirties and forties were asked, "What is your idea of a perfect evening?" Would you believe only 7 percent responded "romance and making love"? Eighty-nine percent said they were stressed out some or most of the time. No wonder their love lives were near the bottom of the list![1]

What's the answer? Katy Koontz, staff psychologist at the Cleveland Clinic Foundation's Center for Sexual Function, offers this insight in a *Reader's Digest* article: "We expect people will fall in love, be each other's best friends for life, and have passionate sex every night. But this ideal for marriage is impossible. It's best to think more about quality than quantity."[2]

To reignite that spark in your love life, think quality, not quantity. Pace yourself. Make arrangements to spend quality time alone with your spouse—time when you can talk about your desires and expectations, really listen to each other, and enjoy uninterrupted intimacy. And be practical! For example, one of the best things you can do to reignite your love life is take a nap. We actually have advised couples to have a sleep date. Get away for twenty-four hours, but spend the first part sleeping. Then you'll be refreshed and ready to fan that flickering spark. Another suggestion is to spend some time pampering yourself in a hot bath. Then you'll be more likely to want to pamper your partner.

Nurturing Intimacy

In between scheduled times together, you can nurture intimacy by integrating loving habits into your family life. We've already said that it's healthy for your kids to see you flirt with each other. Watching you hug, kiss, and share loving gestures helps relieve their concern that Mom and Dad might get a divorce (sadly, one of the major fears of children today). So when your children roll their eyes as you give your spouse a big kiss, remember: they need this as much as you do!

Nurturing intimacy when the kids are underfoot isn't always easy, but here are some suggestions from our survey participants:

- "Touch a lot. We like to hug, kiss, hold hands, and sit next to each other."

- "Court your mate each day in some special way. This definitely boosts our interest in sex!"

- "Laugh a lot."

- "Have your children help plan your date. They pick the baby-sitter and where you go, within reason. Chuck E. Cheese doesn't cut it!"

- "Put your mate first and the children second."

- "Have a weekly date, even if it's just to run errands."

- "Make your bedroom a restricted zone. No entry without permission!"

- "Let your kids know that you love them with all your heart, but they can't consume all your time and energy. Sometimes Mom and Dad need to talk, and they shouldn't interrupt."

The Time and Place for "Quickies"

The term *quickie* can have several different meanings. We mentioned one meaning in the last chapter: a quick sexual encounter that the less-interested partner gives to the more-interested one as a gift of love. It can also be quick sex when both of you are interested but you're pressed for time. Sometimes, during particularly stressful periods, quickies may be all that you can manage; but as long as neither of you feels used, these short encounters can keep love and interest alive until the time when you can enjoy more leisurely, satisfying sex.

Of course, there may be times in your married life when intercourse is not possible or desirable. Yet physical intimacy is still important—maybe even more important. During these times you need to find other ways to bring each other pleasure:

- The last stages of pregnancy
- After the birth of a baby
- When one mate is just too tired
- When one mate is sick or for some other reason doesn't want to have intercourse
- When you need a stress reliever or something to balance your sex drives

Becoming Educated Lovers

Have you heard the old joke about the couple that tried to put into practice some of the communication skills they'd learned in a marriage seminar? While they were in bed together, the wife wanted to help direct her husband's gentle caresses. As he said, "I love you, I love you!" she responded, "Lower!

Lower!" To which he replied in a lower, deeper voice, "I love you! I love you!"

We laugh, but most of us have a lot to learn about love-making. We'd like to be better lovers, but we draw back because of lack of knowledge, inhibitions, past histories, or attitudes inherited in childhood and brought into marriage. Our suggestion? Schedule some time to study sex together. Whether you consider yourself uneducated or well-educated on the subject, you have great potential for learning and growing closer to your spouse in sexual intimacy. Sometimes you just need to be reminded of what you already know!

When our boys were quite young, we designated Monday mornings as our time. We had flexible schedules and could both take Monday mornings off, so we took advantage of a Mom's Day Out program, kindergarten, and school to sched-ule two hours alone each Monday. For those two hours, we didn't answer the door or the phone. We made ourselves unavailable to anything or anybody so we could be totally available to each other. That was our time to learn how to be great lovers. Years later, we are still reaping benefits from those Monday mornings.

Even though our schedules have changed, we have still continued to schedule time for "sex education." Becoming great lovers is an acquired skill. Some people, we suppose, are "naturals," but we have always considered ourselves learn-ers. What we know today about sex is not because we're nat-urally great lovers. Instead, we're great lovers because of what we know and have learned about sex!

What has motivated us to develop sexual expertise? Well, I have always had a thirst for knowledge and an adventurous spirit, while Dave has always had a strong sex drive. Then there's our work in marriage education. If you're going to write and teach about marriage and sex, you've got to do the research.

When we were writing our first book *Ten Dates for Mates*, we read every marriage book we could get our hands on.[3] We talked to every couple who would talk to us. Then, after we researched a subject, we experimented. Some things we liked, so we repeated them. Some things we didn't like. (Chocolate syrup is messy; whipped cream is great!)

Here are three keys we discovered:

Learn How to Harmonize

The sexual experience is like two unique musical instruments harmonizing together, playing a beautiful song that both can enjoy. The instruments are different and respond in different ways to touch and stimulation. In the initial stage of lovemaking, the wife needs gentle caresses. While the husband may respond to a drumroll, she is more likely to respond to the quietly plucked strings of a classical guitar.

Both instruments don't have to sound the high note at the same time. In any great musical performance, there are many crescendos. In fact, the wife may prefer to reach her high notes before her husband reaches his (something that the husband can facilitate in a number of specific ways). At times, one instrument may take the lead in the song, and vice versa. By discovering how to please each other in different ways, you'll eventually develop your own special harmony.

For Husbands Only

You can increase your wife's pleasure. To learn how, we recommend *The Gift of Sex* by Clifford and Joyce Penner.[4] Women can learn how to be orgasmic and even multiorgasmic. While you may think, "That's not fair!" stop and consider the advantages for you:

- It raises the stakes for your wife.
- It creates more interest.
- It benefits you and doubles your pleasure.

—Dave

Be a Lifelong Learner

There is always something new to learn. Just remember that not everything written in books is necessarily true or appropriate for you and your mate. Your most important sex organ is your brain—so talk, talk, talk! Educate each other. Tell your lover what you like and what you don't like. Be willing to experiment and explore.

Set Guidelines for Experimentation

"Our love life can be playful, serious, or very intense, depending on the mood," writes one husband who participated in our survey. "While I have a much greater desire for sexual variety and exploration than my wife, we have learned how to pleasure each other. The greatest stress is keeping our sex life fun and keeping it from becoming routine."

Exploring and experimenting sexually is a great way to invigorate a flickering love life. If you and your spouse agree beforehand on what is acceptable to both of you, you can relax and enjoy it. We suggest adopting the following guidelines:

- It must be mutually acceptable to both of you.

For Wives Only

Don't let sex become just another job or responsibility. The rewards you'll receive from learning how to respond to your husband are worth all the time and effort you put into it. Don't bypass your emotions; even if you're not able or don't want to reach a climax each time you have a loving interlude, stay connected emotionally to your mate. Be transparent, and don't ever fake a response. Give yourself permission to be a sexual person, to have feelings, to surrender to your husband, and to embrace sexual adventure!

—Claudia

- Each of you must always seek to please the other.

- You must have privacy whenever you are exploring and experimenting.

- You must talk openly about whatever you are trying (otherwise, it's easy to misunderstand each other).

Are you ready to revitalize your love life? Then begin talking about your needs and expectations. Review the Love à la Carte menu in chapter 9. Read, learn, and practice. Focus on pleasing one another. Be creative, and pull out that calendar! It's time to start scheduling some sex.

chapter
11

magical minimoments

From time to time we join our friends Kevin Leman and Randy Carlson on their nationally syndicated radio program *Parent Talk.* During one of our visits, Kevin and Randy asked listeners to call in and tell us how they've managed to keep the romance in their marriage through the busy parenting years.

One listener shared a great story: "Our tenth anniversary was coming up and our finances were really limited, so I went to a florist and asked for twelve long stems," the woman told us. "Without the roses, the stems were free! Then I went to the grocery store and bought twelve Snickers bars—my husband's favorite candy. On each long stem, I tied a candy bar with a red bow. Viola! On our anniversary I presented him with a homemade card and a dozen long-stemmed Snickers bars. He'll always remember that anniversary!"

That's just one of the fun ideas we've heard on *Parent Talk*. Randy, Kevin, and their guests are always full of great tips and quips for parents. We like this one from Kevin, which is also the title of one of his books: "Sex begins in the kitchen." He has five kids and a great relationship with his wife, Sandy, so he must know!

What does he mean by "Sex begins in the kitchen"? Kevin believes that your love life begins wherever you are. It encompasses all that you are and all that you do. Sex is played out in a marriage within the context of the whole relationship. Picking up a dishtowel in the kitchen and asking, "How was your day?" affects your love life. Turning off the TV in the living room and talking instead of zoning out affects your love life. The key is to have an attitude that says, "I'm interested in you. I love you. And I look forward to our next time of intimacy and physical closeness."

Such an attitude is expressed through little acts of kindness and innuendoes throughout the course of each day. It's expressed in what we call the "minimoments" of daily life. As the full title of Kevin's book explains, *Sex Begins in the Kitchen: Because Love Is an All Day Affair.*[1]

Whether you have sixty seconds with your spouse or sixty minutes, you can find little ways to improve your love life in relatively brief amounts of time. Through the rest of this chapter, we want to share with you many of the best "minimoment" tips we've collected from participants in our seminars and surveys, readers of our marriage columns, and visitors to our Web site (www.marriagealive.com). We've categorized these tips to make it easy for you to pick and choose. Chuckle at the ones that are too far-out for your taste, and try the ones that feel good to you.

In the Morning

- Kiss good morning.

- Spend your first minutes awake cuddling in bed with nondemand touching.

- Make a cup of tea or coffee for your spouse and bring it to him or her.

- Make your bed together.

- Take complete responsibility for the kids in the morning so your spouse can have extra time to sip coffee, read the paper, or get dressed.

- Bring in a flower from the garden or even a dandelion when you get the morning paper or take out the trash.

- Put the toothpaste on your spouse's toothbrush.

- Kiss good-bye.

- While your spouse is driving to work, call and leave a message on his or her answering machine at the office, saying, "I love you. Have a great day."

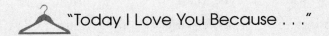 **"Today I Love You Because . . ."**

About three months ago I went to an antique store and bought an old wooden recipe-card box. With a wood burner, I burned my wife's name on top and added some flowers. Then on the front I wrote, "Today I love you because . . ."

Every day since then, I've made a 4"x 6" card for my wife that starts with the words "Today, I love you because . . ." Some reasons are funny; some are serious. Before I leave the house each morning, I leave the card somewhere I know she will find it—in the refrigerator, in her car or purse, or tucked into the morning paper. This exercise has two wonderful benefits. First, it forces me to think hard about why I really do love my wife each day. And second, it may take a long time, but by golly, she's going to believe me eventually!

—A Creative Husband

At Work

- Clean out the car and leave a hot cup of coffee in a commuter mug for your spouse's trip to work.

- Make a tape of favorite love songs that your spouse can play in the car or at the office.

- Have pencils made with a special love message, and leave them in your spouse's pencil holder or desk drawer.

- Have a local photo shop make a mouse pad with a picture of the two of you on it, then put it next to your partner's computer.

- Meet for a romantic lunch.

- Send a care package with homemade cookies or treats for the office.

- Send flowers.

- Give your spouse a gift certificate for a service he or she can enjoy during a lunch hour—say, a manicure, pedicure, massage, or shoeshine.

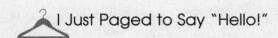

I Just Paged to Say "Hello!"

My husband and I both have pagers. Whenever we're thinking about each other during the day but don't have time to talk on the phone, we page each other with the numbers **07734**, which spells "hello" upside down. When I get that page, I stop and smile. It's nice to be reminded he's thinking about me.

—A Creative Wife

High-Stress Times

- Give a one-minute shoulder rub.

- Brush your spouse's hair.

- Take over some of your mate's usual duties so he or she can escape for a walk around the block.

- Order pizza for dinner.

- Make a joke.

- Give a hand or foot massage.

- Hug.

- Kiss passionately.

- Smile.

- Write a quick love note and slip it in your partner's pocket.

- Go into your bathroom or walk-into closet and hug and kiss until the kids find you.

- Pray together. (As one survey participant said, "This kept us going through five years of sheer terror while raising kids.")

Evening Moments

- Change into something more comfortable.

- Light a candle or two (try scented ones).

- Draw your spouse a bath.

- Finger play while doing dishes together.

- Give away your television (or at least turn it off).

- Snuggle with each other while reading bedtime stories with the kids.

- Eat one dessert with two spoons after the kids are occupied or in bed.

- Rent a romantic video.

Creative Gift Giving

Give each other:

- Matching bathrobes

- Matching coffee cups

- Cell phones so you can always be in touch

- A kite and a trip to the park on a windy day

- A book to share

- Cologne or perfume

- A filled Christmas stocking in July

- Season tickets to a sporting event, the symphony, or the theater

- Hiking boots for long walks in the mountains

- A bouquet of wildflowers

Let Your Marriage Bloom!

Before we were married, I bought my husband a rose-bush. (He is more into gardening than I am.) On each of the branches I put little tags with notes about culti-vating our future love and marriage. I made him read each one before he planted the bush. Now our rose-bush is a reminder of our love and how, with tender-ness, nourishment, and care, it will continue to bloom and grow.

—A Creative Wife

- A picnic basket for two
- A photo album filled with photographs from a favorite vacation

Anytime Ways to Say "I Love You"

Write and send notes, notes, and more notes! Try these:

- Writing an e-mail
- Leaving a voice mail
- Putting notes in drawers
- Tucking notes in briefcases
- Mowing a message in the lawn
- Writing with catsup on a hot dog
- Making a tape of love messages
- Writing a full-length love letter and sending it through the mail

A Welcome-Home Surprise

When one of us is out, the one who is at home sometimes leaves a note on the door to surprise the one who's been away. Once I came home and found a note on the door saying that a hot bath and backrub were waiting inside for me.

—A Happy Survey Participant

- Writing your own love-fortunes and baking them into cookies (The dough can be found at Asian markets.)

Sex-Specific Moments

- Get out the whipped cream or chocolate body paint.
- Develop an "I want you" code that you can use in front of others—something that only the two of you will know.
- Light candles and turn on soft music in your bedroom.
- Give your mate an intimate touch or kiss when the kids aren't looking.
- Offer to take over your spouse's evening chores while he or she takes a bath or otherwise prepares for loving.
- Pull down the covers on the bed and put a candy mint on the pillow.
- Sleep together in the nude.

As you can see, the possibilities for romantic minimoments are virtually endless! Try a few ideas from our lists, or use them to spark ideas of your own. One husband we know put several ideas together to come up with an extra-special minimoment that his satisfied wife will never forget.

"One Saturday afternoon I went out to run errands," she told us. "When I returned I found a trail of notes leading to our bedroom. In the bedroom were two glasses, a bottle of sparkling cider, romantic music, and my husband. The boys were napping, so we enjoyed a romantic interlude!"

Go ahead, be creative! Take advantage of the mini-moments you have with your spouse. You'll find that the "little things" are big when it comes to developing a great love life.

12

getaways to remember

Tony and Erin, parents of three children, managed to survive fourteen years without a single twenty-four-hour period alone together. Tony is a pastor, so weekends are his high-stress, heavy-workload days. Weekend getaways have never been a possibility.

So Tony decided to get creative.

With great excitement, Erin told us how her husband surprised her by making middle-of-the-week reservations for a lovely room with a view at the same hotel where they had spent their honeymoon. He reserved tables for each meal and even arranged for someone to stay with their children. Erin was impressed!

"I felt so loved," she said. "The thought of getting away was a gift as lovely as the actual getaway. Two whole days with no telephone calls, no figuring out which child needed to be where, no driving kids to soccer, no picking kids up from ballet, no preparing dinner for the whole gang or hassling over table manners—just time for Tony and me!"

Rebecca knew her husband, Kyle, was under immense pressure at work. It had been ages since their last getaway, so she decided to do something about it.

"We kept talking about getting away for a weekend, but it just wasn't happening," she explained. "So I decided to take the initiative. I made plans without telling Kyle. Our budget was tight, so I arranged for our two boys to stay with their cousins.

"Kyle's boss liked my idea, so he secretly arranged for Kyle to get off early on Friday. I baked Kyle's favorite chocolate chip cookies and packed the car. Then I drove to his office and kidnapped him! It took time and effort to make all the arrangements, but the look on Kyle's face when he realized what I was doing made it all worth it."

Remembering that day still makes Kyle smile. "I never know what Rebecca is going to do next, but that time she really surprised me," he told us. "On that Friday afternoon, she just showed up at my office and pulled out a blindfold. Everyone in my office knew what was going on except me. The next thing I knew, I was in the car, and she was telling me to relax—that she was kidnapping me for a getaway weekend.

"An hour and a half later, the car stopped. She removed the blindfold, and we were at our favorite mountain lodge in the Smoky Mountains. From that point on, I didn't think even once about all the pressure I was under at the office!"

Tony, Erin, Rebecca, and Kyle know firsthand that pulling off a weekend (or midweek) getaway is a lot of work—but it's well worth it. As each of them discovered, a focused time away from home and routine gives you the opportunity to regroup, reignite romance, and deepen your marital bond.

A getaway doesn't have to be expensive or exotic. It just has to allow the two of you to be alone together for at least a day or two, enjoying each other's company and focusing on loving each other. A successful getaway incorporates these three Ss:

1. *Seclusion.* You need to get away from the pressures of daily life and focus on each other. Leave computers and beepers at home.

2. *Stimulus.* Take along romantic music, a book of love poems, body lotion, bubble bath, your favorite classic romantic video (like *Casablanca*), candles, little gifts, or anything else that would help put you and your spouse in a loving mood.

3. *Sex*. Weekend getaways are a great time to explore and experiment. Bring your favorite how-to book with you or take this book along.

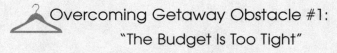

Overcoming Getaway Obstacle #1: "The Budget Is Too Tight"

- Borrow someone else's home or condo for the weekend.
- Clip coupons or watch for specials on hotels, restaurants, and entertainment.
- Check the Internet for cheap, last-minute deals.
- Take food with you so you don't have to eat out all the time.
- Open a special "getaway account" and save up.

—Dave & Claudia

Planning Your Getaway

It takes only one spouse to make arrangements for a getaway; but unless you're planning to kidnap your mate, it's usually best to talk together about your expectations for your time away. Sometimes before a getaway we make a list of things we'd like to do. For instance, I usually look forward to sleeping late and taking life easy. Claudia usually hopes to get in a long walk and start whatever mystery novel has been collecting dust on her night table. We both look forward to making love.

We typically pack a "getaway box" before we go. A getaway box is a designated container in which you put all the little items you want to take on your getaway—things like candles and candle holders, matches, music cassettes or CDs with a player, body oils and bubble bath, your favorite snacks and drinks, your wedding pictures, your favorite devotional guide, and so on. As you place each item in the box, you can think about how much you're going to enjoy romancing your mate. Anticipation is half the fun!

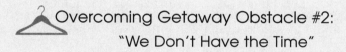

Overcoming Getaway Obstacle #2:
"We Don't Have the Time"

- Don't go for the whole weekend; start with a twenty-four-hour getaway.
- Schedule a getaway on next year's calendar.
- Put "getting away" on the top of your priority list.

—Dave & Claudia

When it comes to planning your getaway, however, be careful: avoid overplanning. You want to come home relaxed, refreshed, and rested, not totally exhausted from an over-structured schedule of "fun." Remember why you wanted to get away in the first place! Don't be discouraged if you arrive at your getaway retreat like most couples do—somewhat exhausted, wondering if all the work of pulling off the getaway was really worth it. Trust us, it is! Here's what other couples have told us about their getaways:

- "Our getaway was more fun than I expected. My favorite part of the weekend was watching an old movie and eating snacks while we were snuggled under the covers. My husband hates crumbs in the bed, so we would never do that at home."

- "We loved holding hands, listening to music, and talking about our memories. We even wrote down our memories to save for posterity. We definitely plan to make weekend getaways part of our future."

- "Our weekend getaway was terrific! We spent a lot of time walking and talking. We even rented mopeds on Saturday afternoon—something we haven't done in years!"

- "We spent hours just talking. We relaxed, ate ice cream, bought T-shirts, and walked barefoot along the beach. We splashed in the cold water and made a decision that we would take up sailing one day. When Sunday came, we didn't want to go home."

As each of these couples realized, marriage is a marathon, not a sprint; and a getaway weekend is not a one-time event. It's something you will want to repeat time and time again. You don't want to feel as though you have a rigid agenda that you must complete. Instead, relax. Have fun. Love each other. Enjoy the comfort of each other's company. Forget about everything else. Do whatever is mutually desirable and pleasing to both of you.

Use your getaway to rekindle that "old spark." Think back to your dating days—to when you first met. Remember when the fires of love and romance were first lit between you. Reminisce and talk about your own unique story. Ask each other what you remember about your:

- First date
- First kiss
- Engagement
- Wedding day
- Honeymoon
- Anniversaries
- Special romantic moments[1]

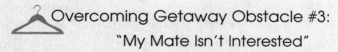 Overcoming Getaway Obstacle #3:
"My Mate Isn't Interested"

- Offer to do all the planning.
- Make your plans around something you know your spouse enjoys, like a sporting event or music concert.
- Arrange a "kidnapping."
- Ask for a getaway as a birthday or anniversary present.

—Dave & Claudia

If you're staying in a hotel, take advantage of the bathtub or Jacuzzi and the toiletry items provided free of charge. Be as creative as you can in your surroundings, and find interesting places or ways to make love.

Favorite Couple Getaways

Getaways can be as varied and unique as the couples who experience them. To help you brainstorm, we want to share with you some of the successful getaways we've heard about from other couples. Here they are, in the words of the happy lovebirds:

Golfing in the Snow Getaway

"One January we hired a sitter to spend the weekend with our toddler and took off for an overnight getaway at a local park lodge. Our room overlooked a frozen lake and snow-covered golf course. On Saturday afternoon, we played a round of winter golf. The whole golf course was ours. As we drove around the course in our golf cart looking for our orange golf balls in the snow, we talked continuously—with no interruptions!"

Timeless Getaway

"It's hard to get my wonderful, workaholic husband to agree to go off on a getaway. But once we get there, he relaxes and enjoys it almost as much as I do. One thing we really enjoy— since we tend to live such structured, time-driven lives—is sleeping late each morning. No travel alarm clocks allowed! We take off our watches and totally ignore the time. If we want to have breakfast at eleven o'clock and lunch at three o'clock, so what? Once we popped popcorn at three o'clock in the morning and fed it to each other in bed!"

Give-Your-Mate-a-Break Getaway

"On our getaway, we experienced romance again. It was a marvelous, freeing experience, like reaching the summit of a mountain! And it was wonderful not to worry about our little interruptions—our three- and five-year-old kids. I was able to relax and concentrate on loving my husband. We took perfumed candles and our portable CD player with our favorite Harry Connick Jr. and Stevie Wonder CDs."

As you can tell, these comments are from a mother with young children. That leads me to offer this reminder to husbands: home may be your castle, but if you have kids, it's your wife's "on location" job site. When our boys were young, the Arp house could best be described as a zoo. At times Claudia, the resident zookeeper and Mama Bear, desperately wanted and needed some time away. As the Papa Bear, all I wanted was my easy chair, a Diet Coke, and a few minutes in the evening in my own little world.

For some time I couldn't understand why Claudia didn't see our house as a haven of rest and a great place for a "stay-at-home" getaway. Finally it dawned on me that, for most moms—even those who work outside the home— relaxing at home is like having a date at work. Right or wrong, mothers simply feel more responsibility to keep the home fires burning—and the noses wiped, and the diapers changed, and the meals on the table. Everywhere they look around the house, they see things waiting to be done. In

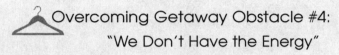

Overcoming Getaway Obstacle #4:
"We Don't Have the Energy"

- Don't go far away—reserve a hotel room in your own town.
- Keep it simple—eat out.
- Plan ahead so there's little to do when the time comes.
- Plan for lots of rest and relaxation, not lots of activities.
- Remind yourself: If you're too tired, you really need it!

—Dave & Claudia

other words, from time to time, home is a place they need to get away from!

So why not take the initiative? Give the mother of your children a break. Plan a weekend getaway for the two of you.

Just think what it will mean to her to have an out-of-home experience!

Looking at the Future Getaway

"One of our most significant getaways was the time we went away for the weekend and looked seriously at our love life and set goals for the future. What worked well for us was to write out our thoughts and desires. We had time to reflect on our marriage and our love life and evaluate our goals and plans—without the kids interrupting and climbing in bed with us," said a survey participant.

Want to have a "Looking at the Future Getaway" of your own? Here are a few conversation starters to help you evaluate your love life and get you thinking about where you want your relationship to go—and how you want it to grow—in the future. Ask one another:

- What are the positive factors about our love life?

- What changes do we need to make to keep our love life fresh and growing?

- What are the resources we can draw on to nurture our love life right now (things like health, faith in God, prayer, finances, time, adequate childcare, and so on)?

- What would an objective observer say are our current priorities? Are these priorities in the right order?

- What role does spiritual intimacy play in our relationship?

- What is our most romantic fantasy? How can we make that fantasy a reality one day?

- What do we want our love life to look like in ten years? In twenty-five years?

Overcoming Getaway Obstacle #5: "There's No One to Keep the Children"

- Swap children with friends—you keep theirs one night, they keep yours another.

- Start a childcare cooperative with other families in your church or community.

- Save up and hire a reliable sitter.

- Recruit relatives.

- Adopt "grandparents," "aunts," and "uncles" from your church or neighborhood.

—Dave & Claudia

Start Fanning Those Flames

Does your love-life battery need a jumpstart? Have the flames of desire in your marriage been reduced to a flicker? If so, you and your spouse need a getaway! Focused, romantic times away from home are wonderful for fanning the fires of intimacy, passion, and marital commitment. They're great at helping you hold on to your love in the midst of work pressures, parenting hassles, and the stresses of daily life. So go ahead, make your plans. Cherish your times away. Fight for them. They're a great investment in your marriage, and we promise they'll do wonders for your love life!

13

the fun factor

During a break in one of our Marriage Alive seminars, a woman named Rachel approached me.

"What did you mean when you said that Dave was your best friend?" she asked. "My husband, Scott, and I have been together for nineteen years. We've had five children together. We love each other, and we work together well. But according to you, we should be best friends. I guess I don't understand what that means."

"Suppose you have a few spare minutes," I responded. "You could use them to tidy up the kitchen, read a magazine, or spend some time with your husband. If you choose to spend time with your husband, you are probably best friends."

Who Is Your Best Friend?

Do you look for ways to spend time with your partner? Do you laugh together? Do you have fun with each other? These are all characteristics of a great friendship. They're also characteristics of a great marriage.

Unfortunately, some couples get so overwhelmed by the cares and concerns of life that they forget to have fun together. They had great fun before they were married. They enjoyed being together when they were dating. That's why they got married in the first place! But it's as if they took a vow of seriousness as soon as they left the altar or as soon as the first baby was born.

In a healthy marriage and love life, it's important to be serious—serious about fun, that is! Can you think of a couple who were best friends and having great fun together who got a divorce? We can't. According to marriage researchers, spending time playing together provides a relaxed kind of intimacy that strengthens a marriage bond. In fact, a recent survey shows that having fun with your spouse is the number one factor for ensuring overall marital happiness.[1]

Becoming Best Friends

If the "fun quotient" in your marriage is low, stop and ask yourself why. Perhaps you take yourself too seriously. Or are you too busy to make time for fun? Maybe you think that fun is just for kids. Maybe it never even occurs to you to have fun.

Just like working on your love life (or developing any worthwhile habit, for that matter), learning to have fun with your spouse takes commitment and an investment of time. You *can* become best friends with your mate. Best friends enjoy the same activities; they love to talk with each other; they love to joke around together. Fortunately, you can nurture each of these aspects of friendship if they're not already present in your marriage.

Do Things Together

If you feel distance in your relationship—if you no longer play together like you did when you first met and fell in love—start setting aside some "couple time" each week to develop a shared interest, activity, or sport. Learn to line dance or square dance. Reserve court time at a local tennis facility. Buy a subscription to a season of theater or opera. Join a bridge club. Take a cooking class together.

Here's another idea: Start a Couples Night Out in your church or neighborhood. Not only will you build a closer friendship with your spouse, but you'll help other couples do the same! It's not hard to start a dating club. Just follow these simple steps:

- *Find several like-minded couples.* Think of friends at church, at work, in your parenting class, or in your neighborhood who might be interested in developing more togetherness in marriage.

- *Choose a date night.* It could be once a week or every other week. Even a monthly date night would be worthwhile.

- *Arrange for regular childcare.* This may be the most daunting task. Of course, every couple could get their own individual baby-sitters. But you may want to pool your resources and make things simpler. For example, you could take turns having all the kids at one home and bring in several trusted sitters. If you belong to a parenting support group, you could ask the childcare workers there if they'd be willing to provide childcare for your date nights too. You could even challenge your church to offer free or low-cost childcare once a month so couples in the congregation could have a regular opportunity to fortify their marriages. Keep brainstorming until you find something that works for you.

- *Pick a theme for each date.* This will add fun, keep everyone interested and on target, and help you and your mate develop new, common interests. Check out your local bookstore for idea-filled resources. (For example, our book *10 Great Dates to Energize Your Marriage* has tear-out pages with suggestions for ten dates that have fun, marriage-enriching themes.)

- *Take turns facilitating a "date launch."* Start the evening by getting together with the other couples and spending fifteen or twenty minutes explaining the night's theme. Then encourage one another to go out and have fun! (If you decide to use *10 Great Dates* as your resource, you may want to get the video companion that includes ten "date launch" segments corresponding to each dating theme.) [2]

A Special Challenge to Parents

Your kids will wait while you grab some time to build your marriage—but your marriage won't wait until your kids grow up. Grab some time now to build your friendship with your spouse by having fun together!

—Dave & Claudia

Talk, Talk, Talk

If it seems that you and your spouse never have anything to talk about but work and the kids, it's time to take action. One idea: Form your own reading club, either with just the two of you or with a few friends. Select a book to read at the same time and then set aside an evening to discuss it. Or choose a periodical or newspaper that you both will commit to read, then pick one article to discuss each evening at dinner. Dialogue may be awkward at first, but as long as you encourage each other's thoughts and perspectives instead of tearing them down, you'll eventually get better at the art of conversation.

Here's another idea: Play the Tell Me game. The object is to find out how much you really know about your mate. Most couples talk about everything except themselves, so you may be surprised to discover how much you don't know about your partner's personal likes and dislikes—no matter how long you've been married.

Either one of you can start the game. Ask a question about yourself, then challenge your partner to answer it. For example, say, "Tell me how I would spend an evening if I could do anything I wanted." The topics can range from heavy ("Tell me my position on ecology") to light ("Tell me my favorite flavor of gum"). Here are some other Tell Me questions to help get you started:

- Tell me one subject I would like to study.

- Tell me the book I would most like to read.

- Tell me which place I would visit first in a strange city— the museum or the shopping mall?

- Tell me the name of the funniest person I know.

- Tell me my favorite saying.

- Tell me what color I think I look best in.

Once you get started, you may have trouble stopping. At least you'll be sure to end the game with some new insights about your mate!

Cultivate Humor

Even the most serious among us can find something funny to laugh about every now and then. That's a good thing, because humor is important in a marriage and a family. It sets the tone in the home, helps release tension, builds positive memories, and strengthens relationships. To this day, we have a cat puppet named Humor that we pull out of the drawer when we're in desperate need of a good laugh. Perhaps you've heard the statement "The family that prays together, stays together." We would add, "The family that laughs together, lasts!"

Here are a few pointers for cultivating humor in your home and marriage:

- Notice funny situations at home or at work as you go through your day, and remember to relay them to your spouse the next time you're together. You don't have to be a stand-up comedian to tell a funny story. If you think your delivery is a little dull, just keep at it. You'll get better.

- Don't get so concerned about offending someone or maintaining your composure that you stifle truly funny moments. Lighten up!

- Think about what makes you laugh—a funny movie, a good joke, a bad joke, irony, crazy stunts—and intentionally seek out those things.

- Remember that a change in behavior often brings about a change in attitude. If you take the first step to increase the laughter and fun in your life—if you try to add humor to your marriage in little ways, even when you don't feel like it—your aptitude for humor will increase over time, and so will your enjoyment.

- Expect that some of your efforts won't be appreciated. As you learn more about what your partner finds funny, you'll be able to fine-tune your attempts to tickle his or her funny bone.

Humor Helpers

- Buy a good joke book.
- Cut cartoons out of the paper, and put them on your refrigerator.
- When you get up in the morning, do a silly dance.
- Choose a wild outfit to wear that will keep a smile on your face throughout the day.
- Have a strange breakfast. (Once, Claudia served popcorn!)
- Wear a clown nose.

—Dave & Claudia

For Parents: Celebrate Family Night

We want to add one last suggestion for couples who are parents. Just as we've recommended setting aside one night each week for "couple time," we encourage you to set aside one night a week for a special evening of family fun—kids included. The point is to do something fun as a family and build memories and relationships in the process. Whatever activity you choose, it should be inclusive of all family members, with sufficient time allowed for talking and joking. For example:

- Rent a family-oriented movie, pop popcorn, curl up on the sofa together, then talk about the movie after it's over. Ask: Who was your favorite character? What values did the story teach?

- Have a game night with special snacks and prizes for the winner.

- Cook a meal together. (Homemade pizza is easy, and even young children enjoy playing with the dough and choosing toppings.)

- Get season tickets to see a professional sports team.

- Make a family video production. Let your children videotape you doing something silly like dancing or snuggling on the couch.

When you have fun as a family, the benefits flow to each family member. Having fun together encourages you to interact and stay in touch with each other's lives. Laughing together diffuses tension and helps you keep short accounts with one another.

And there's another benefit. When a home is fun, children are generally happier and more content to let their parents have some alone time. In other words, family fun can be great for your love life!

It Works!

A year after Rachel asked the question about friendship that opened this chapter, she and her husband, Scott, attended another seminar. On the very first day, they both eagerly approached us.

"Remember when I asked you a year ago about what you meant when you said you were each other's best friend? Well, now I know," Rachel beamed. "This past year, Scott and I have become best friends. I stopped being such a perfectionist around the house and chose instead to spend more time with Scott. It worked! In our twenty years together, this last year has been the best—even with teenagers in the house. We've taken the time to be friends and have fun together. It has absolutely energized our love life and added freshness and romance to our relationship."

We could tell by the sparkle in both sets of eyes that she was telling the truth.

Now, what are *you* waiting for? Let the fun begin!

chapter

14

the six secrets of
highly satisfied lovers

The dinner was exquisite. The atmosphere, romantic. The setting? A thirteenth-century castle, situated high on a hill over-
looking the medieval town of Esslingen, Germany. Sharing
the evening with us were our good friends, Dankfried and
Dorothea. Between the two couples, we had logged over fifty-
three years of marriage! Our discussion of what marriage was
probably like in the thirteenth century gave way to a conversation about marriage today.

"What's happening to marriage here in Germany is dis-
turbing," Dankfried told us. "Even before couples are married,
most lack the commitment to love each other for a lifetime."
He went on to explain that in many modern marriage liturgies,
German couples no longer promise to stay together "until

death do us part." Instead, they promise to stay married "until our love dies."

How sad! Vows like that make divorce seem almost inevitable. But the problem goes beyond divorce statistics. How many couples in Germany—and the United States, for that matter—remain married for a lifetime but experience the premature death of their love life? Love and intimacy grow in stages. When couples ignore their sexual relationship at any stage, it can shut down and die.

What's the Secret?

How can you keep the flame of love burning through all the years of marriage? How can you stay happily married for a lifetime?

When we conducted our survey on love, sex, and marriage, we encountered many couples who, against incredible odds, are finding time to build a creative love life. They're finding time for sex. As we tabulated the survey, we observed that these happy, sexually fulfilled couples have several traits in common. They all know and put into practice what we call the Six Secrets of Highly Satisfied Lovers. We've actually talked about the principles behind each of these secrets throughout the pages of this book. Let's summarize them now.

Secret #1: They're Intentional about Marriage

The marriage of a highly satisfied couple doesn't just happen; both partners are intentional about it. They are committed to each other and to finding time for intimacy and love. They make time to dream and plan together. Even though they are time-pressured, they are in control of their time; time doesn't control them. They intentionally say no to less important commitments that would push them into overload.

Over the years and through many stages of marriage, we discovered that our sex life progressed or regressed in direct proportion to the attention we gave it. At every stage we've needed to be intentional about our love life. We still have to be intentional—even now, in our empty nest.

The Spanish poet Antonio Machado wrote, "I thought the fire was out in my fireplace; I stirred the ashes, and I burned my hands."[1]

Highly satisfied lovers have learned how to "stir the ashes" and keep the fire of love alive. They know how to rekindle the romance and intimacy in their relationship. You, too, can fan the flames of romance with love, patience, persistence, and

Benefits of Building a Creative Love Life

- It will help to "affair proof" your marriage.
- You and your spouse will stay emotionally connected.
- You will be better able to handle stress.
- You'll enjoy better health. (Sex is good for you!)
- You will be a good role model for your children.
- You'll still have a love life after the kids leave home.

—Dave & Claudia

good humor. But you must make the choice. If you choose to have an intentional marriage, you can keep your love alive and growing for many, many years. It's up to you.

Secret #2: They Practice Forgiveness and Acceptance

"I'm the one who is committed to the marriage," one survey participant complained to us. "I'm the one who wants a love life. I can't say the same thing about my husband. I don't think he could ever be romantic, and I don't think he even cares."

Maybe you identify with this woman. Maybe you struggle with many things about your spouse's personality or behavior. The truth is, marriage always involves living with someone who is less than perfect. We've certainly learned that over the years. We hate to admit it, but we still let each other down. We are continually challenged to forgive and accept each other. In our marriage, forgiveness is the oil that lubricates our love relationship.

Fortunately, forgiveness and acceptance can begin with one heart. If you choose to forgive, accept, and concentrate on the positive attributes you see in your spouse, you give your spouse the freedom to grow and change. Along with forgiveness and acceptance let us encourage you to practice compassion, kindness, humility, gentleness and patience (Colossians 3:12). Then you can truly "Bear with each other and forgive whatever grievances you may have against one another.

Forgive as the Lord forgave you. And over all these virtues put on love, which blinds them all together in perfect unity" (Colossians 3:13).

Another survey participant shared how she came to understand this principle. "I've been married for eleven years and have a seven-year-old and two preschoolers," she wrote. "Recently, I've had to come to grips with the fact that my husband is not the romantic, sweep-me-off-my-feet, answer-to-all-my-problems, Prince Charming type. Neither is he abusive, alcoholic, or a workaholic maniac. He is a quiet, hard-working, unassuming, even-keeled man taking care of his responsibilities day by day.

"I'm more the idealistic, romantic dreamer. In the past, whenever I had the chance, I would give my husband articles and books about 'putting romance in your marriage.' He'd finally try an idea, then find it awkward and drop it. I would become very discouraged. Then I began to realize I was asking him to be something he's not, never has been, and probably never will be.

"During our courtship, I was the note writer, the gift sender, the surprise planner. And at that time, I didn't seem to mind his lack of romanticism. In fact, I was attracted to his solid, no-nonsense, logical, realistic grip on life. It balanced my own up-and-down moodiness and emotional view of life. Why is it that the very thing I was attracted to during courtship has become so irritating now?

"It has been a process, but I have come to accept who my husband really is—not what my romantic expectations would make him out to be. I have learned that sometimes you have to accept and deal with your own circumstances and not complain or envy others who seem to be in more 'ideal' situations. I need to keep doing what I can do—and that's my contribution to our love life and marriage."

Do you see yourself in this woman's comments? Perhaps the revitalization of your love life needs to start with *you*. It only takes one partner's positive attitude and action to begin to move a couple forward. Little baby steps taken in good faith can make a tremendous difference. If there is something you need to forgive or ask for forgiveness for, do it now. Then commit yourself to doing everything that's within your power to build a loving relationship with your spouse that will last a lifetime.

Secret #3: They Concentrate on the Positive

This same wife wrote: "I found that I had been dwelling on the negatives and inwardly degrading my husband to such a point that I was unhappy in our marriage. I'm trying now to accept him as he is and look for the strengths, not the weaknesses. On Sundays he's not the dynamic leader up front at church—he's sitting next to me in the pew looking at books with our four-year-old. He's not out leading a men's Bible study or the local Boy Scout troop—he's in the backyard assembling a swing set. He's not the head of a company earning lots of money—he's home every night at six to eat with us and bathe the kids to give me a break. He'll never be a Tom Cruise or Brad Pitt, but he is loving in his own quiet way."

Why not pause right now and make a list of all the positive traits you see in your mate? Concentrating on them will help you build a more satisfying love life.

Secret #4: They Have Fun Together

Happy, satisfied partners have developed the habit of dating. They know how to have fun. They have a sense of humor about themselves and truly enjoy being together. They are each other's best friend. Can you say the same about your spouse?

Secret #5: They Cherish and Nurture Their Marriage

Happy couples cherish their marriage. What do we mean by cherish? To cherish something means to hold it dear, to nurture it, to celebrate it. And while cherishing is a natural outgrowth of a healthy relationship, it can also be intentionally developed.

Practice verbalizing your love and commitment to one another. Demonstrate that love in little, meaningful ways on a regular basis—and in big, spectacular ways every now and then. Nurture your love life by reading books, attending seminars, and educating yourselves on how to become better mates and lovers. Encourage each other and affirm your relationship in private and in public. Finally, celebrate your love for one another. You'll be glad you did!

Secret #6: They Make Time for Sex

Highly satisfied lovers know that a great love life isn't just a matter of *finding* time for sex. They *make* time for sex! Their love life is a priority, and they don't let other activities or commitments crowd it out.

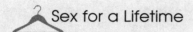 Sex for a Lifetime

Even though my husband is seventy-nine and I'm seventy-six, sex is still fun. We love to have our children visit us for a day or two; but when they leave, I put the red satin sheets on the waterbed, turn on some soft music, and don my sexiest nightie. Then, let the fun begin! Believe me, "faking it" isn't necessary!

—Happy Honey in Honolulu to "Dear Abby"[2]

Seize the Day

As we come to the close of this book, we can't help but think once again about our own marriage of forty-plus years. We have bravely given you a glimpse into our love relationship—one that isn't perfect, one that still struggles at times. We've logged years and years as lovers: Lovers as newlyweds. Lovers as parents. Lovers working together in a profession. Empty nest lovers. And we've arrived at this point in life still cherishing one another and celebrating our love together.

Without a doubt, the parenting years were the most challenging ones for keeping our love alive. Our home is much quieter now, but every now and then our precious grandkids come to visit and fill it with the wonderful sounds of childhood. We see again the stresses, strains, and joys of parenting through the bloodshot eyes of our own children. Our wish for them is that they'll seize the day—that in the midst of their hectic lives, they'll make time for loving each other.

That's something we still have to do. Even now in the empty nest, we find ourselves fighting the "no time for sex" battle. But we've learned from experience that it's a battle worth fighting—and a battle we can win.

You can win the battle too! Never again tell yourself, "There's no time for sex." Instead, use the strategies we've laid out in this book. Adapt our ideas to fit your own circumstances. Try some of the suggestions offered by our seminar and survey participants. *Make* time for sex.

Seize the day!

notes

chapter 1: living in a time-starved world

1. Bill Doherty, "Taming the Time-Eaters—Work, Hobbies, TV and Internet," *Threshold Magazine*, 79 (December 2003), 3.
2. We drew the participants for our "Love, Marriage, and Sex" survey from many of the Marriage Alive and parenting seminars we led around the country over the last few years, as well as from our Web site, www.marriagealive.com. We received over two hundred written responses. All names have been changed to protect the privacy of the participants.
3. Michele Weiner Davis, *The Sex-Starved Marriage* (New York: Simon & Schuster, 2003), 8.

chapter 2: what is a love life anyway?

1. Judith Wallerstein and Sandra Blakeslee, *The Good Marriage* (Boston, New York: Houghton Mifflin, 1995), 192.

chapter 3: revive us again!

1. Paul Pearsall, *Super Marital Sex* (New York: Doubleday & Co., Inc., 1987), 28–29.
2. Ellen Kreidman, *Is There Sex after Kids?* (New York: St. Martin's Paperbacks, 1993), 79–80.

chapter 4: building blocks for great sex

1. Song of Songs 1:15; 2:16; 4:3; 4:5; 4:11; 4:15; 4:16; 5:14; 5:16.

2. David and Vera Mace, *Close Companions* (New York: Continuum, 1982), 96.

3. David Mace, *Love and Anger in Marriage* (Grand Rapids: Zondervan, 1982). This book may be ordered from the Association of Couples in Marriage Enrichment, PO Box 10596, Winston Salem, NC 27108, or by calling 1-800-634-8325. We are grateful to David and Vera Mace for their input into our lives and marriage. Our basic philosophy on how to deal with anger and conflict is adapted from our training with the Maces and is used with their permission.

4. Howard Markman, Scott Stanley, and Susan Blumberg, *Fighting for Your Marriage* (San Francisco: Jossey-Bass, 1994). Drs. Markman, Stanley, and Blumberg are marital researchers and founders of PREP (The Prevention and Relationship Enhancement Program). PREP is a research-based approach to teaching couples how to communicate effectively, work as a team to solve problems, manage conflicts without damaging closeness, and preserve and enhance commitment and friendship. The PREP approach is based on twenty years of research in the field of marital health and success, with much of the specific research conducted at the University of Denver over the past fifteen years. For more information about PREP write to: PREP, Inc., PO Box 102530, Denver, CO 80250, or call: 1-303-759-9931. http://www.prepinc.com.

5. John Gottman, PhD, *Why Marriages Succeed or Fail* (New York: Simon & Schuster, 1994), 29.

6. Pearsall, *Super Marital Sex*, 217.

7. William Macklin, "Making Sex a Spiritual Experience," *Lexington Herald-Leader* (15 February 1997), Today section, 10.

8. Ibid.

9. "Marriage in America," Council on Families in America, 1995, Institute for American Values, 7.

chapter 5: expectations: getting on the same page

1. Davis, *The Sex-Starved Marriage*, 4.

chapter 6: the time-challenged marriage

1. Edwin Kiester Jr. and Sally Valente Kiester, "Sex after Thirty-Five— Why It's Different, Why It Can Be Better," *Reader's Digest* (November 1995), 14.

2. Pearsall, *Super Marital Sex*, 16.

3. David and Claudia Arp, *10 Great Dates to Energize Your Marriage* (Grand Rapids: Zondervan, 1997) and *52 Fantastic Dates for You and Your Mate* (Nashville: Thomas Nelson, 1992, 2004). Both are available through our Web site at www.marriagealive.com.

chapter 7: the energy-challenged marriage

1. Patricia Sprinkle, *Children Who Do Too Little* (Grand Rapids: Zondervan, 1996).

2. Adapted from Jean Lush with Pamela Vredevelt, *Mothers & Sons* (Old Tappan, N.J.: Fleming H. Revell, 1988).

chapter 8: putting marriage first: tips for parents

1. David and Claudia Arp, *Suddenly They're 13—or the Art of Hugging a Cactus* (Grand Rapids: Zondervan, 1999).

chapter 9: love à la carte

1. Dr. Clifford and Joyce Penner, *52 Ways to Have Fun, Fantastic Sex* (Nashville: Thomas Nelson, 1994), 73.

chapter 10: scheduling sex

1. "Idea of a Perfect Evening," *Ladies Home Journal* (November 1994), 52.

2. Katy Koontz, "Is There Sex After Children?" *Reader's Digest* (February 1997), 34–35.

3. Dave and Claudia Arp, *Ten Dates for Mates* (Nashville: Thomas Nelson, 1983).

4. Dr. Clifford and Joyce Penner, *The Gift of Sex* (Nashville: W Publishing Group, 1997).

chapter 11: magical minimoments

1. Kevin Leman, *Sex Begins In The Kitchen: Because Love Is An All Day Affair* (Grand Rapids: Fleming H. Revell, 1999).

chapter 12: getaways to remember

1. Adapted from Arp, *10 Great Dates*.

chapter 13: the fun factor

1. Markman, Stanley, and Blumberg, *Fighting for Your Marriage* (Jossey-Bass, 2001), 250.

2. The *10 Great Dates* video curriculum draws upon the best tips from our Marriage Alive seminars and helps spark fresh romance through memory-making evenings built on key, marriage-enriching themes. These fun, focused dates will help you communicate better, resolve

conflicts, set realistic goals, encourage one another, enrich your love life, develop spiritual intimacy, balance busy lifestyles, and more! For more information or to order, visit www.marriagealive.com.

chapter 14: the six secrets of highly satisfied lovers

1. Gabriel Calvo, *Face to Face* (St. Paul: International Marriage Encounter, 1988), 106.
2. "Dear Abby," *Knoxville News-Sentinel* (16 September 1991), B4.

about marriage alive
international, inc.

Marriage Alive International, Inc., founded by husband-wife team Claudia Arp and David Arp, MSW, is a nonprofit marriage and family enrichment ministry dedicated to providing resources, seminars, and training to empower churches to help build better marriages and families. Marriage Alive also works with community organizations, the military, schools, and businesses.

The Arps are marriage-and-family educators and have been involved in an international marriage ministry for more than twenty-five years. Their Marriage Alive seminar is popular across the United States and in Europe.

The mission of *Marriage Alive* is to train and empower leaders who invest in others by building strong marriage and family relationships through the integration of biblical truth, contemporary research, practical application, and fun.

Marriage Alive Resources and Services include:

- Marriage and family books in eight languages
- Video-based educational programs including 10 *Great Dates to Energize Your Marriage* and *Second Half of Marriage*

- Marriage, pre-marriage, and parenting seminars including Marriage Alive and Second Half of Marriage seminars

- Consulting, training, leadership development, coaching and mentoring

- Contact Marriage Alive at www.marriagealive.com or (888) 690-6667

- Sign up for the free Marriage Builder e-mail newsletter at www.marriagealive.com

Other Resources from David and Claudia Arp include:

Books

10 Great Dates to Energize Your Marriage

10 Great Dates Before You Say "I Do"

10 Great Dates for Empty Nesters

Loving Your Relatives

The Second Half of Marriage

Fighting for Your Empty Nest Marriage

New Baby Stress

Answering the 8 Cries of the Spirited Child

Suddenly They're 13!

Quiet Whispers from God's Heart for Couples

52 Fantastic Dates for You and Your Mate

Marriage Moments

Family Moments

The Big Book of Family Fun

Video Curriculum

10 Great Dates to Energize Your Marriage

The Second Half of Marriage

PEP Groups for Moms

PEP Groups for Parents of Teens